RUNNING
INTO
YOURSELF

RUNNING INTO YOURSELF

JEAN-PAUL BÉDARD

breakaway books
halcottsville, new york
2016

ISBN: 978-1-62124-022-8
Library of Congress Control Number: 2016935643

Published by Breakaway Books
P.O. Box 24
Halcottsville, NY 12438
www.breakawaybooks.com

FIRST EDITION

Contents

The one constant in my life has always been running. It's seen me at my best, and delivered me from my worst. This book is dedicated to all those who have nourished my love of running and to those who have reminded me that greatness is not something we run toward, but rather something that unfolds inside us. But most of all, this is for Mary-Anne, who has always given me the space and love to run into myself.

Preface

The obsession with running is really an obsession with the potential for more and more life.   —George Sheehan

I think we can all agree that life moves faster with each passing day, and how ironic that with the arrival of every modern timesaving device, we appear to be that much farther behind. Everyone seems to be desperately searching for something, but none of us is quite sure what really is gnawing at us, the source of that indiscernible ache. But what if that mysterious thing we are all searching for lies closer than we think?

There is a beautiful story from the Jewish tradition contained within the sacred text of the Talmud. According to the scripture, when we are in our mother's womb, each of us is visited by an angel, and it is this angel who bestows on us all the infinite knowledge of the universe—everything we will ever need to know during our time on this earth. Sadly, just before we are born into this world, once again we are visited by the angel who taps us gently beneath our nose, thus leaving a subtle indentation on our upper lip. This indentation is known as a philtrum, and it is this simple tap that empties our memory of the infinite wisdom we were blessed with in utero. And therein lies the universality of our humanness—a never-ending quest to breathe anew that which once lay inside each of us.

When it comes to a metaphor for this quest that lies at the heart of our humanness, you'd be hard-pressed to find one better than running. There is something primal and pristine about running in that it has the ability to unlock parts of us that otherwise lie dormant, the parts of us that recede farther into the shadows. You need only watch the unbridled freedom of a group of children at play to witness firsthand the joy and expansive beauty of running. There is alchemy in running, as it unleashes us and reveals us.

When you run, you enter into a pact with yourself, whereby in return for having the faith to put one foot stoically in front of the other, not only are you given the opportunity to move away from wherever you might be, but if you are so attuned, you are afforded the rare chance to return to that sacred part that was lost in an angel's gentle touch.

It makes no difference whether you're a novice runner making your way from the couch to your first 5K race, or an elite runner toeing the line at the start of the Olympic marathon. Within the beauty of movement, every runner will inevitably arrive at that mysterious point where he or she must brush up against the same artificial boundary—a space in which we valiantly try to quiet the mind while allaying what at times can feel like incapacitating doubts and fears. This subtle negotiation, this dance with discomfort, is the birthplace of an inner fortitude that demands we keep moving even when everything inside us is screaming for us to quit.

Before we set out on this journey together, I should tell you that this is by no means a conventional book on running. Within these pages, you will not find training plans, dietary advice, or even strength-building exercises. In fact, most of our attention will not be on how to run farther and faster, but instead on how to run deeper. The first part of the book will invite you into the world of a high-profile endurance athlete, a veteran of over a hundred marathons and ultramarathons; an inspirational account of how running has intersected at critical times in his life to help him overcome battles with addiction and personal trauma. We will then turn to how running is a form of moving meditation, a means to not only alleviate stress but also unlock a wellspring of creativity. Interspersed with personal accounts from runners around the globe, we will delve into the archaeology of running and its ability to unearth what may have lain dormant inside us for years.

Next, by drawing on the latest studies in medicine and psychology, we will look into the merits of running as a form of healing and its place alongside pharmacology and therapy. Through real-life stories of athletes who have overcome incredible odds and adversity, we will enter into a discussion of running as a means to strengthen our resilience. If you stick with running long enough, there inevitably comes a time when the wheels fall off and either injuries or life circumstances get in the way of your ability to run. In this section of the book, we will touch upon the perennial issues of running injuries, serious illness, and that oh-so-difficult task of making space for running in your life. And finally, John Donne once said, "No man is an island," so our discussion would be incomplete were we not to look into the importance of building your running tribe as a means to staying motivated and making a positive contribution to the running community in general.

My hope is that within the pages of this book, you will discover much that resonates with that part of you that may have lain quietly waiting in the shadows—but most of all, that you will arrive at a place where running can bring an immense sense of joy to your life. It is a journey that will take you through the pure pursuit of the horizons of possibility within you, and beyond you.

A Dance with Discomfort

How very little can be done under the spirit of fear.
—Florence Nightingale

I've never been one for boxes, let alone putting myself into one. With each passing year, the more I'm inclined to define myself by the fluidity of change, the more I take solace in its slippery elusiveness.

For as long as I can remember, my days have been governed by an insatiable desire for kinetic movement. It has been the unifying thread—the one rhythmic pulse that has been my faithful companion throughout life's joys and sorrows, its growths and transgressions. I'm under no illusion that exercise, which for me comes in the form of running, is in itself either fun or relaxing. But like most things in life, patience and mastery bear the rich fruits of reward.

Over the course of this book, I hope to convince you that if you devote yourself to nurturing a sustained running practice, you will begin to see the positive way it can rewire your brain and awaken your body. More important, you will unlock a wellspring of blissful energy that will rush through you and around you, an energy with which you will become more adept at navigating the world of risk taking and problem solving—two beacons that lie at the crossroads to personal transformation and fulfillment.

Last year I stumbled across an idea that I think beautifully articulates what I've never been able to put into words. The Celtic Christians believed that there were mystical spaces called thin places—the elusive spaces where the veil between the holy and the human is traversed. These are mystical places in which for a brief moment, we humans can clearly see that the physical and spiritual worlds are intricately knit together. Most of us unknowingly walk among these spaces every day, but fail to take notice of their presence. Think of an errant loose thread hanging from the sleeve of a shirt; it's not until you take the time to tug on it that you begin to grasp how it winds its way around you.

Thin places hold such deep resonance and meaning not because they are sacred places, or even peaceful places, but rather because they are places of dissonance, tumultuous transformational plateaus. Upon looking back, I now realize there were indeed times when I was attuned to one of these places. They were times in which the energy that flowed through me was an experience that cleaved my heart open, leaving in its wake a sense of gratitude and awakening.

It could best be described as a disarming feeling of being brought to your own attention, knowing that by being perfectly aligned in this one moment, you are forever changed. It's a disquiet that I'm sure you're familiar with: that tranquil uneasy feeling you are left with when sitting beside a hospital bed watching a loved one take her last breaths, or that feeling of breathlessness that comes upon you when you stand achingly alone on a beach staring out into a never-ending sea.

I think we are predisposed to be somewhat out of sync with these magical spaces because our modern lifestyle dictates that we be constantly active, or should I say, actively preoccupied. And as a result of this unrelenting influx of stimulation and information, it's almost impossible to carve out sufficient time and space to detach long enough to simply unwind and recharge. Instead of cultivating ways of turning off our mind for that much-needed rest, increasingly we choose to numb ourselves with drugs, alcohol, shopping, and food.

Intuitively we know that what we are doing is not working, and I'm rather certain this realization has a lot to do with the growing popularity of yoga, meditation, and other forms of mindfulness. It's as though we've been programmed from birth to always crave more, when in fact it's in the space of emptiness or letting go that we find our greatest fulfillment.

Although it may seem counterintuitive, there is such a thing as good stress, and we can definitely include exercise-induced stress under that category. In his groundbreaking book *Spark*, Dr. John J. Ratey explored the science of exercise and its influence on the human brain. According to Ratey, "The stress of exercise is predictable and controllable because you're initiating the action, and these two variables are key to psychology. With exercise, you gain a sense of mastery and self-confidence. As you develop awareness of your own ability to manage stress and not rely on negative coping mechanisms, you increase your ability to snap out of it, so to speak" (page 89).

And for me, herein lies the essence of long-distance running: In its purest form, it teaches us the art of turning off all that white noise that incessantly rattles around in our mind, and in so doing we heighten our senses to everything else around us. In other words, running is our passport to traverse the boundaries of all those unseen thin places that previously lay outside our awareness.

I can vividly remember one such occasion in which my everyday perception shattered open as I stared directly into the abyss of one of those magical thin places. It was early June, and I was just past the nine-hour mark of what to that point had been the most challenging running event of my life. I had rounded the last turn in downtown Durban and was finally making my way into the Kingsmead Cricket

Grounds for the final few hundred yards to the finish line of the Comrades Marathon, in South Africa. If you're unfamiliar with this race, allow me to set the stage for you.

Imagine if I told you that this ultramarathon requires you to train two to five hours a day, six days a week, spend thousands of dollars, and fly halfway across the world. At which point you would board a ramshackle old school bus, just after midnight, for the two-hour drive to a sleepy village in the middle of South Africa, and all for the pleasure of running what is known as one of the hardest races on the planet. Would you be tempted?

Welcome to the razor-thin edge between sanity and insanity, otherwise known as the world of elite endurance running. The Comrades Marathon is a fifty-six-mile (ninety-kilometer) race up and down unrelenting mountainous terrain across majestic pastoral villages in South Africa. In 2013, I had the pleasure of representing Canada at this race, and up until that time, it was one of the most terrifying things I'd ever done.

So how did I end up in South Africa to begin with?

One of our dearest friends had recently moved to Johannesburg to head up a multinational humanitarian aid organization. We had dinner together when she was back in Toronto visiting family, and she invited my wife and me to stay with her and her wife in JoBurg. I can remember politely smiling as I immediately dismissed the idea. And that was when my friend, Joanna, told me to come down to visit her so that I could run Comrades. Well, to a Type-A, running-obsessed recovering addict like me, there was no bloody way I wasn't flying to South Africa to run this thing. Let's just say the seed had been planted, watered, and harvested—all in a blink of an eye!

The next day I looked into the registration process and set my sights on a marathon in Canada that I could use as a qualifying race. That was the easy part. What I wasn't prepared for was the feeling of impending doom that began to overwhelm me as the deadline to book our flights and accommodation drew nearer.

I consider myself a creature of habit, and I relish the predictability that marathon training and the race itself afford. I love sitting down with a spreadsheet at the start of a training cycle as I scan the benchmarks and key workouts that set out a clear path to my target race. Even more so, I take comfort in the predictable pattern of the marathon—the easy first six miles (ten kilometers) that are run on the nervous energy of excitement, the middle section of the race once my anxiety is quieted and I can adopt a regular even tempo, and the last few miles, the point at which it takes everything in me to will my legs to keep pushing to the finish line.

That being said, everything about Comrades terrified the hell out of me. I had never ventured so far out of my comfort zone before. I couldn't even wrap my head around the race itself because I was so consumed with all the what-ifs. What if after spending thousands of dollars on flights and accommodation, I got injured and couldn't race? What if I had a terrible run and let down all the people rooting for me back in Canada? And then there were all the uncertainties about traveling to a country in flux. South Africa is notorious for its high incidence of sexual violence—was it crazy that I would even risk bringing my wife into this environment?

Mary-Anne managed to be the voice of reason, as she has on so many other occasions in our twenty-eight years together, and she convinced me that it was an opportunity we simply couldn't turn down. So with that pep talk, we decided to make an adventure of it and to fly to JoBurg, with a one-week stopover in Dubai.

The second we got off the plane, we realized we hadn't just stepped out of our comfort zone but had taken a giant leap into a land of make-believe. If you've never seen pictures of Dubai, just imagine something out of *The Jetsons*, with a heavy dose of Disneyland tossed in for good measure. The architecture looked like something dreamed up by Dr. Seuss. Fantastical buildings jutted out, spiraled up, and seemed to defy gravity. Juxtaposed with all the steel, glass, and concrete were the exoskeletons of intricate scaffolds made of bamboo and rope that the migrant workers precariously clung to as they worked to build the latest outcropping of dizzying skyscrapers.

But what I was least prepared for was the intense desert heat. The best way I can describe it is this: Imagine preheating your oven to its highest temperature, and then opening the door and standing in front of it—that's Dubai. It was over a hundred degrees Fahrenheit (forty degrees Celsius) at 2 AM!

By far the funniest part of the trip—though to be honest, it's taken me almost two years to think of it as even remotely funny—was our big "romantic" outing to the desert. In a vain attempt to embrace our newfound nothing-can-scare-us-now attitude, we decided to step completely out of our comfort zone, so we signed up for a one-hour "adventure drive" speeding up and down the sand dunes, followed by an authentic Middle Eastern meal, and belly dancing, in a Bedouin tent set up in the middle of the desert. All of this was to take place under the majestic setting sun.

Well . . . that all sounds idyllic, doesn't it? There's only one problem—I forgot to take into consideration that even under the most ideal circumstances, I have a tendency to get violently carsick. So here I was trapped in a sweltering Land Rover with six other tourists as we bobbed, weaved, and jolted—flying up, down, and around the sand dunes at breakneck speed. Oh, I forgot to mention that our driver divided his time between whizzing tourists around the desert dunes and working as a stunt driver in Hollywood. Let's just say that I think the lines between these two worlds had most definitely been blurred.

Within ten minutes, I had to scream at the driver to stop so that I could get out and vomit all over the pristine red desert sand. After I made three failed attempts to get back into the vehicle—only to beg the driver to let me right back out so that I could vomit all over again—I decided I had had enough. I lay my shaking anemic body down on that warm desert floor, and I said to Mary-Anne, "Just leave me here."

Now, for the record, I should probably tell you that dusk was quickly descending, but I could see the lights of the Bedouin tent off in the distance. In my semiconscious nauseous fog, I figured that instead of enduring another ten minutes of unrelenting queasiness, if I could just muster enough energy to get myself back to an upright position, I could set off for the long walk to that tent on foot, completing the adventure on terra firma.

It was at that point that it finally dawned on me that I wasn't in Kansas anymore. The driver looked at us and in his heavily accented but stern English said, "I cannot leave you here alone in the desert. It's going to be pitch black in about fifteen minutes, and that's when all the scorpions will come out."

I don't want to belabor the point here, but that's when my wife—the love of my life, the mother of my son, the one person who has always been there to bail me out—turned to me and said: "Get your ass into that goddamn truck, *now!*" Let's just say the evening didn't get much better after that. I missed the meal, the belly dancing, and the majestic sunset, all for the comfort of stretching out on the floor of the service quarters of the Bedouin compound.

We awoke early the next morning to board a plane to Johannesburg to spend two days with our friends before taking yet another flight to Durban for the Comrades Marathon. Just to make this trip even more epic, I arrived in JoBurg severely dehydrated from my week of training runs in the intense Dubai heat and, dare I mention, the sudden and unceremonious evacuation of my stomach contents all over the desert floor.

With less than forty-eight hours to go before my race, I was sick in bed, desperately taking in as many liters of fluids and electrolytes as my stomach could tolerate. If you'd asked me at this point what it felt like "stepping out of my comfort zone," I probably would have given you an evil death stare.

Thankfully, everything was about to take a turn for the better.

With a field of eighteen thousand participants, Comrades is the world's largest and most prestigious ultramarathon, and most runners would agree it lives us up to its nickname as "The Greatest Footrace on the Planet." Every year, the race alternates direction between an "up" run and a "down" run. This year was a "down" run starting in Pietermaritzburg and finishing in a cricket stadium in the coastal city of Durban.

Comrades draws elite runners from across Africa and, in increasing numbers, from Australia, Great Britain, and North America. But most notably, it's an event that reaches far beyond the lives of its participants. The entire twelve hours of the race is broadcast live, with an average hourly television audience of a million and a half.

In order to compete in Comrades, you first have to qualify for it at another race, and depending on your qualification time, you are seeded in corrals A through H. Unlike most races here in North America, your result is based on gun time, not chip time. But by far the cruelest part of Comrades is its twelve-hour cutoff time. Of the (typically) eighteen thousand elite runners from around the world who participate in this event, three thousand will drop out along the course; of the remaining fifteen thousand, over 80 percent will finish in the last hour of the race. Those who do finish wait around in the cricket stadium for the epic last minute of the race, at which point the entire crowd starts counting down, *Fifty-nine, fifty-eight, fifty-seven . . .*

At exactly twelve hours, three race officials step onto the course and pull a huge rope across the finish area, preventing any other runners from crossing. Every year, hundreds of runners are left devastated on the track of the cricket stadium—their dreams crushed. They are denied the glory of crossing the finish line. They receive no finisher's medal. It's heartbreaking watching the carnage of the limping, shuffling, and crawling runners as they desperately try to get in under the gun. And therein lies the kicker of Comrades: You're not just in a race, you're waging a constant battle against the clock.

The atmosphere at the starting corrals was electric. On a narrow road outside Pietermaritzburg's colonial style city hall, we all huddled around one another trying to preserve body heat as we shivered and shook in the cool predawn. Five minutes before the start, the entire field of eighteen thousand began singing the national anthem followed by a moving rendition of "Shosholoza," a traditional South African folk song that was sung by Ndebele migrant workers as they were toiling away in the South African mines. The haunting song has come to symbolize the tenacity and empowerment of the South African peoples, carving out a new life in the post-apartheid era. Looking around at the other runners in my corral, I could see that I was not the only one wiping away a tear at the majesty of this occasion. The time had finally arrived, and with a gunshot, we all strode off into the cool darkness to the soundtrack of *Chariots of Fire* echoing behind us.

Although my race took place on a "down" run year, it was "down" in name only. The majority of the course follows long, nasty hills as you pass huge yellow markers every kilometer. These markers are even more daunting because instead of the traditional signage I was used to, Comrades counts down from 89 to 1. And let me tell you, that may sound like only a subtle difference, but when you see that 89 towering down at you from the side of the road, you take a big gulp and your knees quiver as it finally dawns on you the magnitude of the task that lies ahead. In my research before the race, I had read that the only flat part of Comrades is the last three hundred meters when you enter the cricket stadium. Truer words have never been spoken, but the one silver lining in all of this is that I'll never be intimidated by the Boston Marathon's Newton Hills ever again.

The South Africans' reverence for the race was quite the spectacle, and villagers lined the streets along the entire course. The ever-present aroma of their barbecues, known as braai, further heightens the festivities. As an international runner, I was assigned a blue race bib, and along with my Team Canada singlet, this meant I was greeted by "Go Canada" the entire race.

The predominantly rural route has you climbing up and down fairly narrow roads past some rather pungent chicken farms until you arrive at the highest point of the course about halfway through. I was aiming to finish in less than nine hours, and at the midway checkpoint I was right on target. The wheels started to fall off with about twenty miles (thirty kilometers) to go—my quads were wobbly like Jell-O and my feet felt like minced meat. The course profile map looks like an erratic ECG. When I was back in Canada training for Comrades, I thought I would have to walk up some of the hills at the later stages of the race. Funny thing is, it was the downhill sections that took the greatest toll on my body. As I walked down the last two hills, each step sent a shuddering burning jolt through my quads. By the time I got into the city of Durban and the last few kilometers, my pace slowed and my gait faltered, until eventually I more closely resembled the Tin Man from *The Wizard of Oz* than I did a nimble-footed runner.

Despite my addled brain not firing on all cylinders, I was able to do a few quick calculations to figure out that my sub-nine-hour goal was quickly slipping out of reach, so I decided to ease into my last hour and soak up the camaraderie of the race itself. I talked to more runners in that last leg of the race than I'd spoken to in all my other marathons combined. On the road into Durban, I started to look at the runners around me not as competitors but as willing participants in one of the most challenging and life-affirming events of our lives.

At long last, I made the turn into the cricket stadium and the last few painful strides toward the finish line. The moment I entered the stadium, I was in awe of the thousands of cheering spectators, and out of nowhere I felt a surge of adrenaline rush through me. I was no longer running on tired legs, but flying on the best drugs I'd ever taken—accomplishment and humility.

Less than seventy-five yards from the finish line I heard Mary-Anne call my name and heard her scream, "Go baby! Go!" It was precisely then that I brushed up against one of those thin places the Celtic Christians were referring to. And as these two worlds collided, I was no longer just a runner, physically and emotionally depleted and struggling to get my breath; rather, I had become the embodiment of hope, redemption, and faith. For the briefest of moments, I was breathing the rarefied air of the gods.

I crossed the finish line at nine hours and twenty-two minutes, at which point I wrapped my arms around Mary-Anne and broke down and sobbed uncontrollably. I heard her whisper into my ear, "Baby, I'm so proud of you." My journey to Comrades had been built on overcoming depression, trauma, addiction, and fear.

But allow me to turn back the clock a bit so that I can tell you where this journey all began . . .

As I sit down to write this, I can't help thinking of how far I've come in my life, both literally and figuratively. I'm cursed with one of those minds that tend to lock onto something, at the cost of everything else, all the while maintaining a laser focus until the next "new thing" comes along. For years, this obsessive way of interacting with the world cost me dearly in terms of relationships, career, and ultimately my mental health. What's striking is that this Achilles' heel of mine is exactly what I've had to rely on to rebuild my life—and the vehicle of that transformation has definitely been running and the running community in general.

I think my journey as a runner is by no means atypical in that it has more closely resembled an archaeological dig than it has an athletic pursuit. I've never been able to put my finger on it, but running is somewhat like alchemy. Something inside us changes, adapts, or realigns when we lose ourselves in the rhythm of our stride. It's as though our cadence unearths and unpacks all the baggage we've carted around with us throughout our life. What we are left with either energizes us, enrages us, or terrifies us, but whatever the case may be, it forces us into the moment.

But I'm getting ahead of myself again . . .

The ultimate question is: What has brought me to this place, a place where running has become so ingrained in my life? Today lacing up my running shoes is as automatic to me as brushing my teeth or having breakfast.

There was most definitely a time when running was simply another chore I had to fit into my day. There never seemed to be an ideal time to get my run in—it either conflicted with something else on my schedule or interfered with mealtime, and as a result it often fell by the wayside. The most important tweak I've made to my training regimen—one that just happens to be the core piece of advice I would offer up to any novice runner—is to get out of bed early each day and get my run in before the rest of my day gets in the way.

For me, this routine reminds me that my daily run recalibrates me and lays the foundation for which I create the rest of my day. You don't even have to tell me what's going through your head right now. I know what you're thinking . . . When my alarm clock goes off at 4:20 AM, especially on a dark, bitterly cold winter's morning, the last thing I feel like doing is heading out the door for yet another training run. But I can promise you this: If you choose to avoid getting into that daily debate with yourself, and just get your ass out the door, you will never be disappointed. If you're anything like me, you may bitch and moan while you're out there, but the second you get back in the house after your run, you will feel more alive and grateful than you went out.

Those particularly cold and nasty runs, the ones you get done even when your motivation is at its lowest—it's those you can draw on in the last few miles of a race, that "death zone" you enter when your brain is screaming at you to quit. Over the years, I've managed to convince myself that there may be people who are faster, younger, and more talented than I am, but there is no one out there who is more determined. And how did I come to that realization? Simple . . . by getting up, getting out, and getting it done. If you're having a difficult time wrapping your head around that type of commitment, it's probably because you're thinking too far into the future, convincing yourself there is no way you could do that day in and day out. The surest way out of that kind of stinkin' thinkin' is to adopt the mantra that many ultramarathoners use: "Run the mile you're in." Don't think about all the miles ahead. Don't think about all the mornings ahead. Just stay in the moment. Just do it for today, and the rest of the miles will follow on their own.

One of the greatest mysteries to me is when this transformation happened—that precise moment when I ceased being a jogger and started to think of myself as a runner. It's hard to deny the fact that right across North America we are in the throes of another running boom. Although average finishing times for the marathon and half marathon have crept up a little, the number of finishers in both events has seen a steady increase year after year. The most popular distance is still the half marathon, and the greatest influx has been seen in the huge numbers of women who have decided to lace up their shoes and join the running community. Of note is the fact that as of 2013, women made up 56 percent of race participants. When we add in ancillary events like the Tough Mudder, Spartan, and adventure races, we begin to zoom the lens out and capture the even broader appeal of our sport.

As I mentioned before, running has become less something I do and more something I am. The moment I began to identify myself as a runner, I unknowingly aligned myself with a vast community of athletes who identify themselves as fellow seekers.

ONCE AN ADDICT...

If you were to look at a snapshot of my life eighteen years ago, you'd see a young man ravaged by a spiraling alcohol and drug addiction, a man fractured in spirit, a man desperate to claw his way out of a soul-destroying depression. I don't think I ever *became* an addict—I was *born* an addict. If you've ever witnessed someone in the throes of an active addiction, you know it's not pretty. In fact, addiction is a shame-fueled cluster bomb that wreaks havoc in the lives of everyone who comes into contact. My life had become an endless parade of secrets, denials, and disappointments. No amount of willpower would allow me to stop drinking and drugging, and like most addicts, I was on a road that led to only one of two places: treatment or death.

I now believe that the essence of who we are has little to do with what happened to us and everything to do with what we make of what happened to us. Unfortunately, it wasn't until many years into my recovery that I came to this realization. In fact, for most of my life I considered the trauma I lived through as a child as the catalyst, or dare I say "justification," for my addictive behavior.

One of the hardest things I had to wrestle with was that in my mind, nothing about me resembled an "alcoholic." That begs the question: What does an alcoholic look like anyway? Before sneaking through the doors of my first AA meeting, I had a fairly clear idea of what I believed that to be. To me, an alcoholic was a disheveled middle-aged dude stumbling about town in food-stained, urine-soaked clothes. The only thing I was certain of was that there was no bloody way I was that guy! How could I be? I hadn't lost everything yet, I still had my full-time job as a teacher, and my wife and son, although sick and tired of all my bullshit, were still in the picture. But as I've heard said many times in AA rooms over the years: Every addict is on a garbage truck on its way to the dump, but there's nothing saying you have stay on that truck all the way to the end—the choice is yours whether or not you get off before the stink overwhelms you.

I finally came to the point where I was sick and tired of being sick and tired. I think Mary-Anne's limit came when she could see that my erratic behavior was adversely affecting our young son. Faced with the ultimatum of losing my family, I reluctantly looked up the number for Alcoholics Anonymous in the phone book, and with the willpower that only the desperate possess, I reached out for help.

Truth be told, all I wanted was for the person on the other end of the line to tell me everything would be okay, and for her to mail me out some do-it-yourself-at-home sobriety pamphlets. As it turns out, it doesn't work that way. If I wanted to get sober, I would need to put in at least as much effort as I had put into drinking and drugging for all those years. The volunteer on the other end of the phone directed me to a meeting later that evening, and as fortune would have it, it was being held literally down the street from our house.

Looking back on it now, there was little doubt I had walked through the doors of that first smoke-filled AA meeting looking for a way out. I would quickly learn that the AA literature describes alcohol as "cunning and baffling." Alcoholism is insidious in that unlike any other illness, even when it is in remission, it continues to enchant the addict by convincing him or her that "This time it will be different. Go ahead, I dare you take that first drink. You can control yourself."

To my mind, alcoholics drink for one reason, and one reason only—to numb the pain buried inside them, and in so doing to valiantly attempt to make their problems go away, even if it's only a temporary reprieve. The bitter irony is that the alcohol, or any drug for that matter, never solves anything. What it does do is mask problems and anesthetize fractured emotions that, given enough time, will bubble their way to the surface like a festering abscess.

I was coming up to my two-year anniversary clean and sober when one evening, Mary-Anne and I were sitting around the with some friends having a big communal meal. Just in passing, one of the men at the table mentioned that he had run a marathon a few months back. Now, there is nothing remarkable about that statement, except that, how do I say this politely, it had come from one of the least athletic-looking people I know. I guess that is just another example of the universe at work, or another fine example of my ingrained prejudice. All these years later, I now realize that runners come in all shapes and sizes, but we all share one thing in common—a desire to reconnect with a part of us that only running can unearth.

Needless to say, all of us sitting around the dinner table were absolutely gobsmacked by the thought of running farther than most of us drive in a day! For the next twenty minutes, our friend regaled us with stories of his long winter training runs along the lakeshore, black and gnarly toenails, chafed nipples, and a long list of chronic aches and pains. The general consensus around the table was that no one in his or her right mind would sign up for that kind of torture. And with that we switched gears and got back to stuffing our faces with the evening's fare.

I went home that night with a gnawing feeling inside me, something that most definitely had a patina of envy to it. In no way did I miss the gut-wrenching vomiting and skull-crushing hangovers that accompanied my drinking days, but boy did I ever long for the chaotic shitstorm of excitement that preceded the inevitable slide into remorse and bitterness. Don't get me wrong, I was ever so grateful that by the grace of God, I'd been able to get a few years of sobriety under my belt, but it's not until you stop drinking and drugging that you begin to realize how much of your time was spent feeding or mopping up after your addiction. The two things I missed most were not being able to take the edge off a bad day with a little buzz, and not having any way to punctuate the start of my weekend by going on a little after-work bender. For me, the mind-numbing thing about sobriety is that each day just blurs into the next. It feels as though there are no high points to the week—both figuratively and literally. A recurrent topic of discussion in 12-step meetings is the addict's insatiable need for self-inflicted chaos. And come to think of it, I would have to say that it's this very fact, a fascination with the torturous edges of chaos and pain, that draws so many recovering addicts into the world of endurance sports.

I most definitely wasn't coming to the running scene as a complete newbie. I had competed in cross-country in my elementary and secondary school days, and even when my drinking was at its worst, many mornings I'd head out for a twenty-five-minute run—usually with a queasy tummy, not to mention dressed head-to-toe in cotton, something I now know is a completely taboo for runners.

About a week after the dinner party, one of the women who was sitting around the table that evening called me up and asked if I'd be interested in joining the half-marathon clinic with her at our local running store. I guess I wasn't the only one whose curiosity was piqued by the dinner conversation. The clinic met one night a week for a brief lecture, followed by a five- to eight-kilometer (three- to five-mile) run around the neighborhood. In addition, every Sunday we were to meet bright and early at the running store for our weekly long run that maxed out at nineteen kilometers (twelve miles).

We were entering the biting cold of mid-January, so it didn't take long to separate the newly minted hard-core runners from those less inclined to expose themselves to frozen water bottles and throbbing fingers, let alone the less attractive possibility of hypothermia and treacherous black ice. Six weeks into the program, those of us still left standing, or should I say limping and aching, religiously followed the training schedule set out in the clinic guidebook. The most critical piece of advice, something that I still believe in to this day, was something referred to as the 10 percent rule—never increase your weekly mileage by more than 10 percent, in order to avoid increased risk of injury. Despite heeding this advice, my partner in crime couldn't shake a nagging Achilles injury, and with less than three weeks to go before our targeted race, she made the wise decision to drop out of the clinic.

Ironically, or maybe even serendipitously, the National Capital Half Marathon took place on Mother's Day. Little did Mary-Anne and I realize at the time that this would be the first of many special occasions in our lives when my running obsession trumped everything else on the calendar. Come to think of it, how fitting that running would now take the place of all those countless weekends lost to hangovers, not to mention all that family time sabotaged by my drinking. I guess it's true what they say—once an addict, always an addict.

I think now is the perfect time for a little aside, in order to give a huge shout-out to the lesser-known heroes of our sport without whom we mere mortals of the running world would be at a loss. The people I'm referring to are none other than what I affectionately call our running Sherpas. Just as highly skilled mountaineers would never contemplate an ascent of Mount Everest without the assistance of trusted Sherpas, adept at the highly technical Himalayan passes, we runners are beholden to those caring individuals who, among other less attractive duties, drive us to and pick us up from races near and far. My wife often jokes that she's not entirely sure when she signed up for this gig, but without a doubt, to my mind she's the best running Sherpa on the planet.

If I had to write a job description for a running Sherpa, it would most likely sound something like this:

Wanted: Faithful Running Sherpa

• *Must be willing to forgo weekends and family time during spring and fall racing seasons*

• *Must be content to wander aimlessly around race expos as your runner weighs the pros and cons entailed in purchasing compression socks versus compression sleeves*

• *Must be content to subsist on a diet that includes eating pasta four nights a week*

• *Must be willing to forgive (or more likely ignore) your runner's inevitable grumpy mood and irritability during the taper period leading up to every race*

• *Must buy in to the idea that 10 PM on a weekend really is a "late night"*

• *Must be adept at standing for hours watching an endless stream of runners while waiting to take the perfect action shot or video of your runner grunting and waddling down the homestretch toward the finish line*

• *Must be amenable to giving your runner a big hug and, if lucky, a big kiss after the race even though your runner is a salty, sweaty, smelly mess*

If you don't already have your very own running Sherpa lined up, I suggest you get cracking on that one as soon as possible, and if you're not sure how to recruit one, let me pass along a little sage advice my wife has on the subject. Pick destination races that offer a great time to check out a new city or country—preferably ones with excellent shopping and fantastic restaurants. Also, if you're not targeting a particular race as your goal race of the season, and there's no hope in hell of you getting on the podium, don't hole up in your hotel room the day before the race saying: "I want to rest my legs." Remember why you started running in the first place, and be grateful for all the incredible things you will discover about yourself along the way. Much of our training is a lonely and isolating activity, so why not embrace the opportunely to share your adventure with those you love? By far my most memorable running experiences were those in which I embraced the camaraderie and festivities of the race itself.

I can remember our instructor telling us in one of our first clinic lectures that you may be able to pull off a 5K or 10K race without putting in the effort of training, but when it comes to the half marathon and marathon, there is absolutely no way you can cheat the distance. Now that I look back on my longevity and success in long-distance running, those words remain paramount in my training and race preparation. At this point, I've run well over a hundred marathons and ultramarathons, but the butterflies in my stomach at the start line of each race are a constant reminder that anything and everything can go right, or wrong, over the course of the distance.

So with my family in tow, I hopped in the car for the five-hour drive to Ottawa for my first half marathon. Race morning arrived with near-perfect running conditions, lots of sun, no wind, and a balmy fourteen degrees Celsius (fifty-seven degrees Fahrenheit). Not surprisingly, I fell into the trap that sabotages most newcomers to racing—I went out too fast, and for the remainder of the race my pacing was all over the map. The final two kilometers (1.2 miles) felt like they stretched out for an eternity, but as I crested the last hill with the finish line in sight, I caught a glimpse of Mary-Anne and Noah standing at the barricade along the finishing straight. Despite my erratic pacing, I managed to cross the finish line in a time of 1:32, shattering my "unannounced" goal time by more than ten minutes.

I could see in Mary-Anne's eyes how proud she was of me, because for the first time in as long as I could remember, I had actually set out to do something, put in the hours of hard work, stuck with my plan, and seen it to fruition. However, I credit what happened next with catapulting me headfirst into my voracious love of long-distance running and for the subsequent huge chasm running has opened in me, allowing years of recessed pain to escape and love to flood in.

After crossing the finishing mat of my first half marathon, I waved to Mary-Anne and Noah as I gingerly made my way down the race chute to receive my hard-earned and much-coveted finisher's medal. I bowed my head so that the young race volunteer could drape the red-and-white ribbon over my head. The weight of that silver medal resting on my chest was the closest I'd ever come to feeling like I was standing on the podium with an Olympic gold medal around my neck. But it wasn't until after I had grabbed a bagel and banana that I first noticed my hard-earned racing hardware was in fact only half a medal. Apparently, just the athletes who completed the 42.2-

kilometer (26.2-mile) marathon distance received a full medal. Hanging around my neck was a crescent-shaped silver medal with jagged edges—it looked as though someone had simply snapped a full medal in half. The joke was literally "on me."

I'm giving the race organizers the benefit of the doubt here because I'm sure it wasn't meant as a malicious design choice, but damn, don't they realize what awarding half a medal does to a Type-A addict like me? I had just dragged my sorry ass farther than I'd ever run before in my life, something that should have been a huge personal accomplishment, but all I could think of was that missing piece. The whole experience brought me right back to my drinking days when I'd crack open that first beer in a case of twenty-four, and instead of focusing on the twenty-three bottles still unopened, all I felt was melancholy as I stared at the one empty. It was at that moment I made a promise to myself that next year, I'd return to get a full goddamn medal!

Another hard-earned lesson I took away from that first half marathon was how critical are the decisions you make in the initial few hours after an endurance event like a marathon or half marathon. I had spent months preparing myself to get to the finish line of my race, but I had given very little thought to what would happen immediately after the race. By the time we got back to our hotel, I felt so beaten up that I could hardly wait to jump into the hot Jacuzzi for a long soak, followed by the greasiest burger I could find, and preferably with my tired ass parked in a recliner for the rest of the day. Well, it turns out that all this pampering and sitting may have felt intoxicating at the time, but in actual fact all I was doing was delaying my recovery and increasing the subsequent day's muscle soreness.

Instead of a hot shower or leisurely soak in a steamy Jacuzzi, what your body really needs is a short, and may I add brutally unpleasant, dip in a frigid ice bath to help bring down the swelling in your muscles and kick-start the healing process. Your brain may be trying to convince you to immobilize your tired legs; however, the best course of action is to ice your legs, get some protein and few carbs into your body as soon as possible, and then head out for a slow forty-five-minute walk to keep your legs moving. Having run more than a hundred marathons, I've become hypervigilant when it comes to race recovery. My wife usually gets me out for a good long walk within two hours of my crossing the finish line. Another suggestion I offer up to those new to marathoning is to do an easy thirty-minute run the morning after a marathon or half marathon. Your cadence in the first ten minutes may more closely resemble the gait of the Tin Man from *The Wizard of Oz* than that of a fleet-footed Kenyan, but believe me, you will thank yourself later that day. This light run flushes out much of the accumulated lactic acid, the culprit for the dreaded DOMS (delayed onset muscle soreness) that tends to cripple most runners in the forty-eight hours after an extreme endurance event. The sooner you get your body accustomed to this post-marathon recovery run, the sooner you can say good-bye to walking downstairs backward and wincing every time you try to sit down.

It took me a good week to recover from that first half marathon, and probably another week before I felt like lacing up my shoes to head out for another run. All of the months spent preparing and training were definitely a distraction from that core restlessness that continued to dog me in my sobriety. There was no doubt in my mind that I was an addict in remission, so the only way I believed I could stay sober was to find another distraction—but for an addict, that means upping the ante to something bigger and better.

It appears that the Fates were looking out for me yet again, because as it turns out, I found the next distraction in the unlikeliest of places—an AA meeting. I'll never forget that Friday night, in late fall, when I was sitting in on yet another closed meeting of Alcoholics Anonymous. As is the case with most 12-step gatherings, the meeting was taking place deep in the bowels of a musty church basement. My mind was wandering as I looked around the room trying to avoid eye contact, when I noticed an older gentleman enter the room. I had seen him around the rooms before, and as on every other occasion, he was wearing a baseball cap, something that he never took off, even indoors during our meetings. As he was walking past me, I caught a glimpse of the back of his windbreaker, and it's only now that I look back on this moment fourteen years later that I realize how greatly the trajectory of my life was changed by this chance encounter. Emblazoned across the back of his jet-black windbreaker was the majestic head of a unicorn, embroidered in gold, and framed by the words BOSTON ATHLETIC ASSOCIATION—BOSTON MARATHON.

For the remainder of that ninety-minute meeting, I sat staring mesmerized at that shimmering golden unicorn and the rich epic tradition it represented. For Christ's sake, it was the Boston Marathon; even people who have never laced up a pair of running shoes have heard of the illustrious race. You know that "should I, shouldn't I?" feeling you get when you see one of your favorite heroes or celebrities out in public, and you struggle with whether you should approach him or her? Well, that's exactly what was racing through my mind as I looked longingly at that jacket. After the meeting finally let out and everyone was mingling on their way to the parking lot, I walked up to the guy wearing the jacket and timidly asked: "So, what's it feel like to run the Boston Marathon?" You'd think a question coming at you like that completely out of the blue would knock you off guard a bit, but that certainly was not the case. I can now attest, from my own experience, that wearing a Boston Marathon jacket around town is just like being seen out in public with a newborn in a snuggly or a cute slobbering puppy—it's like a homing beacon that attracts every stranger on the street, as it gives people the perfect opportunity to strike up a conversation with you.

My life definitely took a turn for the better that night, but it wasn't until I really got to know Bryan that I began to appreciate the ease at which he can hold random strangers captive as he weaves a tale in such engrossing detail that it feels as if you were actually there with him.

Standing by the door leading out of the church basement, Bryan said: "Oh man, you gotta run Boston. It's not just the race that's incredible. It's the whole atmosphere. The entire city is buzzing during marathon weekend. There are over a million spectators along the course, and I swear to God, it's the closest you'll come to feeling like a world-class athlete."

Trying not to come off like a gushing starry-eyed wannabe, I casually said, "Yeah, I was thinking I might sign up for next year's race." And with those words, there was little doubt that I was a complete running novice who was about to have the rug pulled out from under him.

"Really? Have you already qualified for Boston?" Bryan said.

"Qualified? What do you mean, have I already signed up online, or something?" I had absolutely no idea that in order to run Boston, you first must run a fast-enough qualifying time at another marathon based on your age and gender. The conversation quickly turned to a jargon-laced Running 101 lecture about PBs (personal bests), kilometer split times, lactic acid thresholds, and a whole slew of other things I'd never heard of. I could clearly see there was no way I was going to navigate a graceful escape from this conversation, so I reluctantly admitted, "Well, um—I've never actually run a marathon. But I have run a half marathon."

A true testament to the gentleman Bryan is, he patiently answered all my questions, something I construed not only as a kind gesture but also as a clear indication of his deciding to take me under his wing. He told me I'd need to slowly ramp up to longer and longer training runs, and that I would need to pepper in some tempo and hill runs to strengthen my core and cadence. He also mentioned that the Toronto Waterfront Marathon was a perfect initiation to the distance, as it was considered one of the fastest and flattest marathons in North America. In other words, a race that was ripe for one day knocking off a Boston qualifier. Bryan said he was targeting Toronto as his fall marathon, and in his next breath he invited me, a doe-eyed complete novice, to tag along with him and a few other guys for their Sunday long runs on the waterfront trail.

I must have looked like a little kid on Christmas morning as we shook hands and made our way to our respective cars. I had come through the doors of Alcoholics Anonymous to stop drinking; little did I know that it would be one fateful encounter with another runner at a meeting that would be the catalyst to helping me stay sober all these years.

A month into my joining this rogue group of runners for their Sunday long run, two things became apparent: First, if it weren't for our shared love of this sport, there is no bloody way our paths would ever have crossed, and second, when you're suffering, life always feels a little better when you have someone else suffering alongside you.

Before embarking on my running journey, I had no idea how it would nurture my soul in much the same way that my 12-step meetings did. In both instances, I was being immersed in a supportive community that built me up by lovingly tearing me down. The only thing that both communities asked of me was that I show up, be honest, and strive to make the "me of today" just a little better than the "me of yesterday."

With each passing year I'm around the running community, I realize how much our ranks are rife with addicts who have turned to running and triathlons as an integral component of their recovery.

It's been bittersweet to discover that, for me, the silver lining of addiction is to see how the unremitting toll of having spent years of my life destroying myself at the hands of drugs and alcohol has been fertile preparation for the rigorous mental and physical extremes endurance sport demands of my body. The farther you travel down the rabbit hole of addiction, the more you rely on self-delusion to insulate your "self" from the brain's warning signals of pain and self-protection. It feels beautifully ironic to me that this ability to partition off part of my brain almost killed me, and now it's what I draw on to keep me moving forward in the hellish last few miles of a marathon or ultramarathon.

One Sunday, another young gentleman turned up to join us on our two-hour run along the waterfront trail. As is typically the case, after the initial meet and greet each week, our group splits up into smaller packs of three or four people who run at the same pace and—more important—share the same sense of humor. Bryan made sure that this new arrival broke off into our group, and as soon as we got moving I understood why. Jon was also a recovering addict, and he too was training for his first marathon, so this sounded like the perfect fit for our vagabond running group. Ten minutes into my run with Jon, I knew that we would hit it off. Jon is blessed with a wickedly funny sense of humor, dripping with wry sarcasm and self-deprecation. Running for two or three hours at a time can be mind numbing and soul destroying, so it's always an asset having a quick-witted wiseacre in tow to help pass the time. As much as I appreciated Bryan's mentorship, there was always the natural divide of him being a little older and having more sobriety under his belt; Jon and I were similar in age, however, and were both relatively new to navigating a life free from drugs and alcohol.

Looking back on these weekly training runs of two or three hours, I now understand that they were less about making me physically stronger and more about trying to convince myself that I had a deep well of resilience from which I could draw. I can honestly say we didn't spend a lot of time talking about recovery during these long runs along the lake, but as a consequence of following through with my commitment to the other guys in my group to show up week after week, I inadvertently did some much-needed growing up.

The older you become, the less comfortable you feel putting yourself out there and making new friends. One of the incredible gifts that running has given me is the confidence to put myself into unfamiliar situations that consistently provide the opportunity for me to make new friends. Because running is an individual activity that you can do in groups, it operates on the premise of parallel play. This is a universal form of play in which children engage in the same type of activity adjacent to one another, but at no time do they try to influence one another's behavior. Parallel play most often occurs when there is a common interest, and in our case, it happened to be running. I'm sure you've witnessed the phenomenon of children who start off playing adjacent to one another, but eventually begin to engage cooperatively in a shared activity. That's been my experience with running: What begins as a few random strangers meeting up for a group run at a local run club often leads to carpooling to races, having coffee after a workout, and even socializing completely outside of the running environment.

I had spent the majority of my life thinking I was broken and unworthy because I defined myself by all the baggage and trauma I'd been lugging around since my childhood. Running permitted me the canvas to redefine myself, not as a victim of abuse or a recovering addict, but instead as first and foremost a runner—someone who was not afraid of physical challenge and the mental endurance that coincides with that. Week by week, I grew to trust the men in my Sunday run group, and in turn I garnered their respect simply by showing up when I said I would.

Marathon morning had finally arrived, and Mary-Anne, my ever-faithful running Sherpa, agreed to drive Jon and me to the staging area near the start of the marathon in Toronto's downtown core. Jon and I had prearranged to meet up with Bryan on a street corner near the starting line so that we could hang out together before the race and—more important—tap Bryan for some last-minute wisdom and advice before the show got under way.

The butterflies were definitely dancing around in my stomach as it finally dawned on me that, unlike our Sunday runs, I wouldn't have Bryan to rely on to monitor my pace. In order to qualify for the Boston Marathon, I needed a time of 3:15 or better, and based on Bryan's age, his qualifying standard was 3:45. I'd been struggling with pacing issues throughout my training, as typically I would go out too quickly at the start and gradually fade around ninety minutes into my run. Luckily for me, I was completely familiar with the Toronto course profile because we had the opportunity to run large sections of it on our Sunday runs.

Bryan kept hammering away at how important it was to maintain an even pace throughout the entire race. He warned me repeatedly about the trap that so many runners fall into: banking time early in the race. According to this strategy, the first part of your marathon is run at a faster tempo in the hope that you can bank some time for later in the race when your pace begins to float up. It sounds so tempting, which is more than likely why so many novice runners fall prey to this strategy. What usually ends up happening, though, is that you deplete all of your glycogen stores in the first third of the race, leaving your body forced to rely on its ability to process less efficient fat stores for fuel. Compounding that is the dreaded heaviness that begins to creep into your legs from the accelerated lactic acid buildup from the fast tempo in the early stages of the race. This is the physical sensation that runners refer to as hitting the wall in a marathon—that mystical zone where physical endurance and psychological willpower converge. It's a haunting, lonely place to be. Instead of having to break through this threshold at around the twenty- or twenty-two-mile mark (thirty-two- to thirty-five-kilometer), a vain attempt to bank some time early in the race will bring you to this wall at the sixteen-mile (twenty-six-kilometer) point. And believe me, that's a long, long, long way from the finish line.

WRAPPING YOUR BRAIN
AROUND THE DISTANCE

Fast-forward to today, and now that I've run more than a hundred marathons and ultras, I am frequently asked to give talks at various running clinics around the city. I run as few as nine and as many as twelve marathons each year, so as you can imagine the question that comes up most often is "How do you manage to run so many marathons year after year?" I typically respond by saying that for me, running is not an activity I do or a sport I participate in, but rather a relationship I've entered into. Like any relationship, its success is contingent upon trust and respect. I have to trust that if I'm faithful and committed to it, this relationship will be my constant companion in both joyful and tough times. But more important, no matter how many marathons I've run, I must always respect the distance. Like waves rising in the sea, the physical and mental toll of the marathon never diminishes, but with time and a little patience you can become more adept at riding those waves.

I think the best way to wrap your brain around running a marathon is to break the race up into different stages, each with its own peculiarities and intricate milieu. It's often said that your ultimate success at the marathon distance is determined within the first ten kilometers (six miles) of a race. The trick is not to be lulled into the communal buzz and festivities at the start of the race. When the pack begins to thin out around the one-mile (1.6-kilometer) mark, it's very tempting to ignore your game plan and ratchet up the pace. Whatever you do, be careful not to get sucked into running someone else's race.

It's also important to note that at many of the smaller races, the half-marathon runners start at the same time as the marathoners; that too can lead to pacing confusion and disparities at the beginning of a race. To reinforce the importance of starting slow and steady, I like to make a mental note of the runners around me whom I suspect are going out too quickly, because I know that in most cases I'll pass each of them later on in the race. When it comes to the marathon, the old fable of the Tortoise and the Hare certainly rings true!

These first few kilometers are all about quieting your nerves and giving your body the space it needs to settle into a comfortable groove. That being said, if you're anything like me, this is also the time at which you become hypersensitive to every little ache and twinge, and the residual wear and tear that comes from logging all those training miles. Unless you have been deluding yourself, and you have indeed arrived at the start line with a serious injury, something that for all intents and purposes should have kept you sidelined, my advice is to consider this state of runner's hypochondria as nothing more than your mind's last-ditch effort to sabotage your plans for what will more than likely be an incredible feat of human endurance.

Over the next twenty minutes or so, as I ease into my allotted pace, I calm my nerves by checking in with each part of my body: Am I holding any tension in my neck? Are my arms comfortably bent at my sides? Am I clenching my hands or squeezing my fingers? I once read that the best way to be sure your hands are in a relaxed position during a race is to imagine that in each hand, you are holding a butterfly by its wings. And finally, I consider whether I am over-striding instead of "floating" each time I push off from the ground. I also find it helpful to repeat the mantra "Run with your legs, not your mind," because this somehow slows my breathing and brings me more in tune with how my body is moving through the moment. Ironically, the mantra I use toward the latter stages of a marathon is the complete opposite. When my physical endurance is waning, I tap into my brain's ability to override my physical faculties so that I can power through to the end of the race despite the shooting pain in my quads and calves.

I like to call the second stage of the race the check-in or check-out stage. This is the point of the race at which you'll have to make an honest—and let me stress that word, *honest*—assessment of whether or not today is your day. The bitter truth of the marathon is that despite all the careful planning and dedicated preparation you put into your training, a multitude of sabotaging factors lie beyond your control on race day. You can never be sure what impact the weather, race logistics, and even digestion will have on your ability to reach your desired time goal. This is the very reason why most seasoned endurance athletes head into a race with an A, B, and C goal. I've seen too many runners blow up in the latter stages of a race—or worse, end up in the medical tent—because they didn't take extreme heat or bone-chilling cold into account during their race.

So if you're fortunate enough to have made it this far, you're now at the halfway point of the race. Naturally, you think you're halfway done, but the truth is that the real race has just begun! This is the time you need to trust in your training and maintain a razor-sharp focus on maintaining two, and only two, things—an even cadence, and strict hydration and fueling. By "an even cadence" I mean maintaining a consistent effort that takes into account the potential fluctuations of the course profile. There is no need to charge up a hill; all you have to do is maintain the same perceived effort that you had on the flats. Because most of us run with GPS watches, we are spoiled by the access to constant real-time data. When it comes to calculating your pace, think in terms of longer sections of one or two kilometers (0.6 to 1.2 miles) rather than trying to lock into one pace the entire time.

I've had the pleasure of working as an official pacer in quite a few marathons over the years, and what I've noticed every time is that what started off as a chatty group in the first half of the race inevitably becomes a quiet and robotic group of zombies somewhere around the twenty-five-kilometer (fifteen-mile) marker. That's not very surprising considering that this is the point at which your brain is consumed with enlisting all the systems required for your body to survive the physical hell you're putting it through. My advice to those new to the marathon is that this is precisely the time you should do anything possible to distract your mind from sabotaging your forward momentum. If I'm pacing a group, this is when I bring out amusing running anecdotes or long drawn-out stories about some of the epic races I've participated in around the world, all with the purpose of redirecting everyone's attention outward.

I don't think most of us take up running to win races and retire on the prize money and endorsement deals. I truly believe that every runner is an ambassador for our sport but—more important—that it is our duty to show others the joy that comes from moving the body and releasing the mind. So this is the point in a marathon when you should look for kids along the route offering high-fives, scan the crowd for some funny homemade signs, or even strike up a little conversation with the person running beside you.

We have now entered the most dreaded stage of the marathon, ripe with its lore and tall tales, that death zone known affectionately as hitting the wall. Truth be told, it's really not that scary after all—it just feels foreign to us because our training plans rarely have us exceeding thirty-six kilometers (twenty-two miles) in the buildup to the marathon. I can vividly recall the self-doubt that overwhelmed me when I hit this point of my first marathon. From novice to elite, every runner reaches this daunting barrier where your body basically runs out of gas as you go into big-time glycogen debt.

As I mentioned before, your body relies on fat for fuel throughout most of an endurance event like a marathon, but it's the glycogen that acts as the fire to burn that fat, so any dramatic decrease in glycogen stores leads to a catastrophic sequence of events. The muscles in your legs suddenly become less pliable with each passing step, and as you begin to seize up, no amount of willpower can assuage a significant drop in your cadence.

As if the physiological deterioration is not enough, the neurological signals kick in and begin to wreak havoc on your mental perception. Every signal dispatched from your brain is screaming at you to slow down or risk death. What really distinguishes elite athletes from the rest of us mere mortals is their uncanny ability to mute those sabotaging brain signals that nature has hardwired into our brain as a self-protection mechanism. Along with our innate flight-or-fight response, our minds are wired to preempt any perceived internal damage to our body by signaling the need to respond to the physical onslaught it is under. What's important to remember is that the human brain is predisposed to kick in much sooner than is actually necessary to forestall any catastrophic physical damage. Therefore, in order to achieve the greatest success in the marathon, an athlete must become intimately acquainted with this zone of dissonance—this razor-thin line that demarcates maximum performance and utter catastrophe.

Over the years, I've flirted with various strategies in my training in an attempt to push the wall back, with the hope that it appears later in the race. I wouldn't recommend upping a few of your long runs to the full marathon distance; the extra wear and tear on your body might leave you prone to injury or, worse, sidelined. A safer way of mimicking how your body feels when it hits the wall is to add in a few back-to-back long runs during your training. You might try running thirty-six kilometers (twenty-two miles) on Saturday, followed by twenty-five kilometers (fifteen miles) on Sunday. What this does is get your brain used to running on tired legs. Another strategy is to run the last five kilometers (three miles) of your long run at a little faster than your race pace. Believe me when I tell you this really does a number on your mind. It's the closest I've come to replicating that mind–body dissonance of the latter stages of a marathon. And finally, I often deprive myself of any gels or other fuel in the last hour of my long run. This is an excellent way to get your body accustomed to running on fat stores rather than on the more efficient fuel of carbohydrates. But I should add that if you decide to play with your fuel intake like this on some of your long runs, make sure you replenish your protein and carbohydrate stores within thirty minutes of completing your training run.

IS THAT BOSTON OFF
IN THE DISTANCE?

I had arrived at the turnaround point out in Toronto's west end. All that was remaining in my first marathon was the eight-kilometer (five-mile) stretch along the freeway back toward the downtown core. I'll never forget that feeling of euphoria I had knowing that I was about to nail my A-goal of qualifying for the Boston Marathon in my first race! With about thirty-five minutes of racing remaining, and all of it along a familiar route I had run with the boys every Sunday for the past six months, I was nothing short of ecstatic. But then the harsh reality of the marathon reared its ugly head. Like Icarus flying too close to the sun, I was brought crashing back down to earth. My legs began to seize up, and my heart rate suddenly shot up from 155 to 180. I could see my dreams of Boston slipping away with every second, and every torturous compulsion running through my brain was begging me to walk, stop, or lie down.

That oxygen-rich blood that had so effortlessly been coursing through my quads now felt like thick treacle, and with every tender truncated step, my hamstrings knotted up more as my gait began to shorten. This race took place quite a few years ago, so it followed the old Toronto Waterfront Marathon course. At the time of my first marathon, this hellish death zone in the course appeared at a particularly industrial and isolated section of the city. With the motorway shut down for the race, the runners slowly banked upward on an elevated freeway ramp before making the turn into downtown and the final mile of the marathon. Feeling nauseous and dizzy, I looked down at my watch as I tried in vain to determine whether or not a Boston qualifying time was still in the cards. My math skills barely rival a third grader's at the best of times, so it didn't take me long to realize that with my oxygen-depleted brain, there was no way on God's green earth I could determine the pace I'd need to pull it off.

Forgive me if I sound as though I'm whining and whingeing; I know there isn't a lot of sympathy out there for us runners who willingly fork over a lot of money to put ourselves through this masochistic ordeal. But I have to say I learned more about fear and my untapped reserves of strength in the gruesome last twenty minutes of my first marathon than I had from having survived physical and sexual trauma as a child and, later, suicidal depression and addiction as an adult. I learned that if you focus and dig deep—and I mean big-time subterranean digging—it really is possible to silence your brain and take it completely out of the equation; to tell it, "Shut the fuck up because I'm not listening!"

But it wasn't until I broke out of the final turn and made my way along Front Street toward the screaming crowd and the red-and-white arch above the finish line that I truly grasped the lore of the marathon and why it holds so many people in its web. With each of those final strides, I shed a little of the emotional baggage I'd been carting around with me for years. I have no doubt that I had spent the majority of my life running away from something, but now I could see a possibility of one day running into myself.

I crossed the finish line of my first marathon in a time of 3:11. Holy shit, I had qualified for Boston. And for this addict, I had just sucked up the biggest endorphin high on the planet, and I was already jonesing for my next hit.

THE HOLY GRAIL
OF LONG-DISTANCE RUNNING

Whether it's a painter trying to capture the vast emptiness of a shadow in a fading sunset, a sculptor attempting to tease out the essence of beauty lying encased within a slab of granite, or even a poet desperate to land upon that perfect phrase to envelop the depths of a lover's eyes, each of us is on the eternal quest to arrive at perfection—and each reminds me of the essence of what it means to be a runner. It's a cautionary tale, and we must tread carefully, as this can be a thankless pursuit that will haunt your dreams and shatter your every waking moment.

We runners are indeed blessed when it comes to this life-affirming odyssey, as we often stumble upon perfection in the unlikeliest of places—be it all alone on the pristine downy snow of an untrodden backwoods trail, or in the glimpse of a mountain peak as we ascend the crest of a summit. Most typically, it arrives with that sudden flood of endorphins that creeps up on us out of nowhere and fills us with a transcendent feeling of euphoria—that ethereal moment when everything just seems to click on an otherwise inconsequential training run.

But when it comes to the sport of running, I think most runners would agree that one of the sweetest elixirs, and perhaps the Holy Grail of long-distance running—the closest we runners ever come to being in the presence of perfection—comes in the waves of emotions that fill you when you nervously wind through the sleepy streets of the little town of Hopkinton, Massachusetts, as you make your way toward the start line of the illustrious Boston Marathon.

Like the poet vainly searching for the phrase that encapsulates the depths of a lover's eyes, arriving in Hopkinton, I too longed for the words to express that elaborate dance of joyfulness and trepidation that percolated through me. There along the undulating road that leads to Boylston Street in downtown Boston, I was standing on sacred ground, a road scattered with lifelong dreams fulfilled, interspersed with countless hopes lying crushed.

It's not until you get off the plane at Logan Airport that you begin to grasp the enormity of the Boston Marathon and how the entire city swoons to make every visitor feel welcome and important. In fact, with the exception of the Super Bowl, it's the largest one-day sporting event in the United States in terms of spectators and media coverage.

Every April, thousands of runners, and their friends and families, descend on the relatively quaint city of Boston—draped out to reflect all its enchanting New England charms. The race falls on Patriot's Day Monday, a holiday in Maine and Massachusetts. The few days leading up to the race see the downtown core awash with some of the best runners on the planet.

Perhaps the most visible tradition unfolds each year at the race expo, where runners line up to purchase the annual commemorative race jacket, usually designed in a dazzlingly bright color. It's the very same jacket that caught my eye in that AA meeting many months before, and it's the one coveted item that every Boston runner desperately wants to own. Walking around the streets of downtown Boston on the weekend leading up to the race, you look out on a mass of runners all wearing the same garish race jacket.

During my first weekend in Boston, every conversation, every meeting, and every meal was about running, and nothing but running.

Time felt like it just flew by and the big day was quickly drawing near. After a restless night of anxiously checking the alarm clock every fifteen minutes, I crawled out of bed hoping that by starting my pre-race preparations, I would somehow quiet the butterflies tap dancing their way around my tummy. Marathon morning had arrived!

The Boston Marathon is primarily a straight 26.2-mile (42.2-kilometer) run from Hopkinton to downtown Boston. Because accommodations are scarce in the little town of Hopkinton, on race day the majority of the runners begin filing out of their hotel rooms in downtown Boston in the wee morning hours. I had arranged to meet up with a few other runners from Toronto outside the hotel so that we could make our way through the deserted streets, most of which had already been cordoned off for spectators who would line the route later that day. The designated bus boarding area is situated on Tremont Street, bordering on historic Boston Common, a site most fitting considering it has come to represent the indomitable will of the human spirit and the nation that grew out of its turbulent colonial past.

When it comes to race logistics, the Boston organizers certainly have their hands full. Having to transport almost thirty thousand runners twenty-six miles to the start of the race is no easy feat. As a runner, you can anticipate having to wait at the staging area in Hopkinton for close to three hours prior to the race. You also have to take into account the somewhat predictable unpredictability that arrives with springtime in New England. Further complicating matters, and born of the security concerns that have only increased in recent years, is that the runners are only allowed to carry a small plastic bag with everything they will need in terms of food and clothing for the three-hour wait at the start.

And so, waiting to board the convoy of yellow school buses, and snugly wrapped in an array of old sweatshirts, leggings, and a mishmash of plastic bags and duct tape, the sleepy runners fell into the long lines forming at the edge of Boston Common.

The bumpy bus trip out to Hopkinton felt like it took an eternity, and the whole time all I could think about was that I had to run this entire way back to Boston. I've been fortunate enough to return to Boston ten times over my running career, and every year I'm back, I look forward to scanning the faces of the other runners on my bus as I try to pick out the first-timers, the veterans staring off into the distance contemplating whether today is the day they have a PB in their legs, and finally those fidgeting and squirming in their seats because their overzealous hydration has left them with an achingly full bladder and the knowledge that there is no Porta-Potty in sight for at least an hour!

After the sixty-minute drive and an additional thirty minutes required in order to clear the backlog of buses at the arrival area, I shuffled out of the rickety school bus and joined the long cue of runners snaking their way to the huge grassy fields known as athletes' village. I had been warned by Boston veterans that the first thing on my agenda was to zero in on an empty plot of grass so that I could lay out my plastic tarp and throwaway blanket and thus claim my own piece of real estate on the muddy embankment of the school yard—my home for the next three hours.

Anyone who has run a marathon is well aware that one of the more stressful parts of marathon day is something that is rarely discussed and something that receives very little press—the delicate art of bladder and bowel evacuation. The palpable air of anxiety, in conjunction with the shivering early-morning springtime chill, makes for a lot of loose tummies and overactive bladders. Bearing that in mind, you now probably have an idea of how the thirty thousand runners spend their three-hour wait in Boston's athletes' village prior to the start of the marathon. That's right . . . we're lining up for the Porta-

Potties, and if you're smart, when you finally do get to the front of the lineup and take care of business, you'll turn right around and join the back of that line to start the process all over again.

With an hour to go before the official start time, the runners begin to abandon their piece of grassy real estate and embark on the fifteen-minute walk to the corrals at the start line. I have to say it's quite something seeing thousands of runners shuffle along the narrow residential street as they pass the town's picturesque historic clapboard houses on their way to their assigned starting corrals. The solemnity of the entire experience can't be overstated, and what's more, there is an odd dichotomy of runners, some who look like they can barely contain their joyful awe, while others appear as somber as if they were taking their last lonely walk to the gallows.

The corrals are lined up one after the other as far as the eye can see along Main Street, in the bucolic New England town of Hopkinton. Runners are assigned their corral seeding based on a qualifying time, with the fastest runners placed toward the front of the race. Once we had each filed into our respective corrals, we stood shoulder-to-shoulder huddling up to preserve our body heat in the chilly spring air. At this point, it's safe to say that the same thought was coursing through every runner's mind: *I wish I had gotten one more pee out.* With the minutes winding down to the firing of the official starting gun, the final announcements and introductions of the elite athletes echoed over the loudspeakers strung along the street.

Immediately following the announcements, the runners were asked to take off their caps for the singing of the national anthem. I can tell you that growing up in Canada, I have heard the American anthem sung hundreds of times in movies and at sporting events, but it wasn't until I had the opportunity to sing the anthem myself and witness firsthand the Americans' pride that I fully understood the beauty and majesty of those lyrics. And with the crescendo of the anthem, and right on cue, an F-16 soared just above our heads on a flyby. With my heart in my throat and my legs quivering, I took one final look around at the sea of runners. Everything felt incredibly surreal—here I was about to run the Boston Marathon!

If you were to sit down and talk to me about running, it wouldn't take long for the conversation to tilt toward my unabashed love affair with the people of Boston and with the hordes of runners who descend on that beautiful seaport city to compete in the Boston Marathon year after year. Since running the race for the first time, I've had the pleasure of returning on many occasions to take in the splendor of Boston's historic streets lined with stunning cherry blossoms, and the added privilege of making the pilgrimage from Hopkinton to Boylston Street. Having said that, I'm under no illusion: Boston is definitely not the kind of race that loves you back. In fact, its legendary terrain chews you up and spits you right back out again. It's the hope of every runner who lines up in Hopkinton to leave a little gas in the tank for the latter stages of the race when you hit the marathon's notorious Newton Hills, the most famous being Heartbreak Hill. And let's be honest, those hills can suck your will to live and leave you gasping for breath as you crest each one, only to arrive at the base of yet another climb.

When it comes to training for Boston, most runners will inevitably include a healthy dose of hill repeats in their training plans in order to be ready for the thunderous onslaught of the Newton Hills. Having run Boston over ten times, I'm convinced that the most challenging part of the course may not be the rolling Newton Hills, but rather the long and misleadingly steep descent that begins just after you cross the timing mats at the start of the course. As I prepared for my first few Boston marathons, veterans of the course continually warned me to be careful in the first five kilometers (three miles), and suggested that the key to a successful Boston is to hold back the pace in the first 20 percent of the race to lessen the pounding on my quads during that unrelenting downhill section. After the first time I ran Boston, I was on such a high from having completed the historic race, and in a fairly respectable time, that I just dismissed the advice from the veterans: To me, that early downhill section appeared to be a non-factor. Over the next few years, I never gave these critical initial few miles of the race the respect they deserved. What continued to puzzle me was that despite all the winter hill training I threw into my preparation for the race, every spring my careful race preparation was derailed, time and time again, by those goddamn Newton Hills.

Here's the problem . . . when that starting pistol is fired, you're so jazzed up on adrenaline and the buzz of the crowd that your pace naturally accelerates, and during the first mile or so of the race it feels as though you're floating effortlessly down the hill. You can be warned about this, and read about it all you want, but until you experience the race firsthand, it's difficult to understand how narrow the road is during the first section of the course and how easy it is to get sucked up in the enthusiasm of the crowd. Getting an accurate read of the pitch of the terrain is further complicated by the fact that both sides of the road are lined with screaming spectators three or four people deep, and it continues like that all the way out of Hopkinton.

In 2014, the year after the tragic bombings, I ran the Boston Marathon twice in the same day—something known as a Double Boston. I started in downtown Boston early on marathon morning and ran the 26.2 miles out the start line in Hopkinton. I timed it so that I had about forty-five minutes to wait around in my corral, and then I turned around and ran the official marathon with the rest of the athletes. Other than being one of the most physically challenging things I'd ever done, the experience of running the course in reverse, with no other athletes or spectators along the route, afforded me the opportunity to really see the terrain up close and personal. The funny thing is, I hardly noticed the Newton Hills when I attacked them in the opposite direction, but when I got to the last 5K leading into Hopkinton, I realized how long and steep the first section of the course really is. No wonder my quads are always beaten up and pretty much useless by the halfway point of the Boston Marathon. Yah, I know what you're thinking: *This guy really is a slow learner.* It may have taken me ten races to accept the advice the veterans had given me all those years ago, but in my defense, once I buy into something, I'd rather die trying than admit I may be wrong.

My advice now to anyone training for Boston would be to include a lot of downhill repeats in your marathon training plan. What typically happens when we runners do hill repeats in training is that we charge up the hill, and then either jog or walk back down to prepare for another round. I'd suggest tweaking this routine somewhat, by dropping the pace on the uphill climb and then going a little harder on the downhill. This will get your quads used to the pounding of the first section of the Boston course.

I also recommend incorporating some hill work (approximately five to ten kilometers, or three to six miles) at the beginning of your weekly long run on at least three or four runs starting about two months before Boston. This is an excellent workout to simulate what your legs will feel like as they get used to a sustained effort after an early downhill pounding. As with any training suggestion, let your body be your guide. The workout and training benefit is pointless if it leaves you with a nagging injury heading into Boston.

As I stood in my corral at the start of my first Boston Marathon, all the months of preparation had distilled into one magical moment, and I had the rumbles in my stomach to prove it. And with the shattering *BANG* of the starter's pistol, we were off. Well, you know what they say about the "best-laid plans . . ." It took all of five seconds for me to realize that any hope of easing myself into the race had flown out the window. The shit just got real—and by that I mean real fast. Before I knew it, the first twenty minutes of the race had flown by in a chaotic frenzy as thousands of runners jostled for position on the narrow undulating road.

For me, the first few miles of any race always fill me with dread because in the confusion of everyone cutting in and out as they try to move up in the field as quickly as possible, I'm terrified of being tripped up or having someone clip my heel. In my opinion, this initial marathon frenzy is even worse in Boston because everyone in the race is seeded in corrals based on their qualifying time; as a result, even relatively fast runners who are used to lining up at the start of the pack in their local races might find themselves five, six, or seven corrals back in Boston.

Like most races, Boston relies on chip time rather than gun time for official results, but if you're seeded in one of the rear corrals it might take four or five minutes after the gun goes off before you reach the starting mats. I think this "dead time" takes a heavy psychological toll on the runners, as it creates a sense of panic over a time deficit that needs to be clawed back early in the race. Every year I run Boston I see literally hundreds of runners sprinting, dodging, and weaving their way through the congested pack in the first few miles. No doubt, many of those runners are falling into the trap of trying to bank time early to make up for the inevitable slowing of pace in the Newton Hills; or quite possibly they are trying to catch up to friends seeded in a corral or two ahead of them. In either case, it's safe to say that any success they had expected to achieve on this day pretty much ended in those first few fateful miles. It's easy to underestimate how much energy all this skirting in and out at an accelerated tempo requires from you, and it's not until you have come crashing down to earth after the initial adrenaline rush that you begin to see your race plans slipping away from you.

Definitely one of the highlights of the Boston course comes at around the twelve-mile mark (about nineteen kilometers) as you approach the thunderous screams, whistles, and cheers emanating from Wellesley College. It makes no difference how much you're in the zone; at about a mile out from Wellesley, you can hear the clanging of cowbells and the high-pitched screaming off in the distance, and as you draw nearer the college, the noise becomes almost deafening. Every year, the Wellesley women line the narrow street of the marathon en masse; their collective screams and cheers are a much-needed shot of adrenaline for the weary runners, who are all getting ready to lock into survival mode for the second half of the race.

As they line the low barricade along course, many of the young women hold up handmade signs saying things like KISS ME, I'M GERMAN, or KISS ME, I'M A CHEM MAJOR, or, my particular favorite, KISS ME, I PROMISE I BRUSHED MY TEETH! Well, you get the idea: Here you are halfway into the Boston Marathon, the mother of all marathons, the day you've spent months and quite possibly years training for, and now you're being asked to slow down, stop, and kiss a complete stranger. How crazy awesome is that! The first time I ran the Boston Marathon I blew right past this fun-fueled mob because there was no way I was going to sacrifice precious seconds to kiss a stranger. Turns out that was but one more rookie mistake.

I've been fortunate enough to run the Boston Marathon many times now, and the record I'm most proud of is not my fastest time on the course, but last year's race when I managed to get a total of fourteen kisses from the ladies of Wellesley College. And let me explain why Wellesley's carnival atmosphere couldn't come at better time of the race. Perhaps my biggest pet peeve about the running boom has been the increase in the number of runners who run with iPods and other listening devices in races. I think it's one thing to rely on music to distract you on a long, lonely training run out in the winter's cold, or on a treadmill at the gym, but in my opinion, zoning out with a headset in a race is not only counter to the essence of the race itself but also a missed opportunity to embrace the complete racing experience. When you're competing in a large marathon like Boston, Chicago, or New York, you can count on having to spend most of the race in the midst of a congested pack of runners. It's critical for your own safety, and that of the runners around you, to be aware of where you are at all times. When you run in a music bubble, you are unaware of your surroundings, and thus prone to wander in front of another runner. Don't believe me? Next race you're at, watch what happens on the approach to a water or aid station. Invariably, someone wearing a headset decides to stop without warning or dart in front of another runner in order to grab some hydration. It's reminiscent of those old cartoons with Mr. Magoo—people bouncing around the course completely oblivious to the chaos they leave in their wake.

And let me just counter the argument put forth by those who say that listening to music during a race motivates them or, for many, offers a reprieve or a much-needed distraction from the discomfort of the marathon. If you really want to get motivated, try running a race without your head lost in music. In so doing, you'll be able to hear the screams of encouragement from the crowds along the course, the gentle commiseration and support from the runners around you, and—most important—the echo of your footsteps and the rush of oxygen in and out of your lungs.

So all of this brings me back to the thrill of running through the cacophony of support known as Wellesley College. When you tune yourself in to the unwavering energy and enthusiasm of these young ladies screaming their lungs out, you can't help but be reminded of why you took up running in the first place. I'm fairly certain you didn't start running so that you could knock off a PB in every race, or to masochistically put your body through the rigors of unimaginable pain. Most of us came to running because it unlocked a feeling of freedom and joy that somehow reminds us of the innocence of our childhood. I truly believe running has little to do with getting from one place to another as quickly as possible, and everything to do with returning to a place of joy within us.

And I guess that's why I feel that the exuberance of Wellesley College couldn't come at a better time in the race. Every time I reach this milestone in the Boston Marathon, I'm immediately snapped out of my own little world of self-obsessed self-importance, and I'm reminded of all the gifts running has brought into my life. Even if you don't stop for a kiss, I guarantee you that you'll be buzzing for at least a mile or two after the din of Wellesley College fades off into the distance behind you.

After smiling for the photographers at the halfway point, I now faced the nastiest section of the marathon on the horizon—those unrelenting Newton Hills were the only thing standing in the way of me getting my hands on that coveted Boston Marathon finisher's medal. Considering the many hills I've encountered in other races and in training runs, the Newton Hills are not that steep in comparison. What makes them so challenging is their steady, long ascents, with very little reprieve to catch your breath between each of the climbs. This section of the course is always well populated by cheering crowds of spectators, so any thoughts you might have of walking up the last few meters of each hill are quickly put to rest. If you tap into the energy of those spectators, I guarantee you'll find the willpower to forge your way up each nasty hill. No matter how many times I run the Boston course, I still can't keep track of which hill I'm on and of how many climbs remain. You'd think by now I'd be more adept at navigating the course, but by the time I get to this section of the marathon, my oxygen-depleted brain is definitely not firing on all cylinders.

After pounding my way up Heartbreak Hill and cresting the final incline, like most of the runners, I was all but spent, but it wasn't long before I caught a glimpse of the iconic CITGO sign off in the distance. Every athlete who laces up to run Boston knows to keep an eye out for the CITGO sign because once you finally reach it, there is only one more mile to go until you hit the finish line. But in keeping with the mantra of most Boston athletes, "If it were easy, everyone would be doing it," the cruel irony of the CITGO sign is that you see it long before you ever get close to it. In fact, there are parts of that course where it appears to your addled brain that the CITGO sign is fading away into the distance rather than getting closer.

The intensity of the crowds really started to ramp up as we got closer to downtown Boston. My running gait certainly wasn't pretty, as my hip flexors had completely seized up and my beaten quads left my legs feeling like Jell-O. In the first few years I ran Boston, unlike nowadays, the race started at noon, so the late start meant that working out race-day nutrition was one part alchemy and one part dumb luck. You don't really want to have a big meal too close to the start of the race; as a result, most runners had their last meal at breakfast before boarding the buses to the athletes' village in Hopkinton. By the time I got to the last few miles of the race, it was almost 3 PM and my stomach was nauseous from all the gels and energy drink sloshing around in there. The only thing keeping me moving forward was the thought of how amazing I would feel walking back to my hotel with a Boston finisher's medal draped around my neck.

I came around the last turn of the race, and the narrow roads I had been running on for the past three hours opened up to the wide expanse of Boylston Street. Nothing could have prepared me for how emotional I would feel seeing the mass of spectators lining the barricades, but far and away the most beautiful sight of all was the majestic blue-and-gold banners that encased the giant scaffolding at the finish.

I grunted my way across the finish line and immediately made my way over to one of the volunteers in the finishing chute so that she could place the solid pewter Boston medal around my neck. Next, I wrapped myself in a shiny silver Mylar warming blanket and joined the sea of other runners shuffling toward the food tables. I'm sure from a distance, in our shiny space-age wraps, we must have looked like something out of NASA. As I dragged my exhausted body toward the baggage buses, two thoughts were going through my over-stimulated yet depleted brain. One, *I just ran the fucking Boston Marathon! Holy shit!* And the second: *That was brutal! I never, never need to do that again!*

Oh, how naive I was!

A Moving Meditation

My desire for knowledge is intermittent, but my desire to bathe my head in atmospheres unknown to my feet is perennial and constant.
—Henry David Thoreau

There is a question that often comes up in conversation with non-runners that rarely seems to come up in conversation with other runners: *What do you think about while you're out there running hour after hour? Don't you go crazy? Aren't you bored silly?*

On the surface, it seems like an innocent enough question, but it's one that I really have to struggle with to find an answer. You see, I love to run, but that's not really why I run. For as long as I can remember, I've waged a not-so-subtle war trying to keep my restless, overactive mind in check. To an outsider, this internal restlessness manifests in my frenetic, and some would say manic, hyperactivity.

My wife says that I have only two speeds: hyperdrive and zonked out. If you do manage to get me sitting in a chair for any length of time, I'll inevitably be twitching, fidgeting, and tapping my feet. I have stopped trying to figure out why I'm like this; I think I'm just wired this way. Over the years, I've attempted to mollify this incessant restlessness with every external means at my disposal, most notably drugs and alcohol, and to a lesser degree food. Although each has offered a temporary reprieve, none has been sustainable for very long, and truth be told, it really is a fool's game because no matter what you do to escape from yourself, sooner or later you are faced with having to return to that you were escaping from to begin with.

As I mentioned before, I don't consider running something I do, but rather something I am. And I believe it's within this oneness with running that I can begin to answer the question of what goes through my mind when I'm out on long runs. If you were to look at my training logs for the past four years, you would find that I average just over nine thousand kilometers (five thousand miles) a year. That's a lot distance covered in the course of year, but it's not until I work out what that equates to in terms of a time commitment that I begin to see how much running really does dominate my life. In the past year alone, my cumulative time running works out to be almost twenty-eight total days (if I were running twenty-four hours a day).

One of my mantras in sobriety has been "Keep It Simple," and it's a philosophy I've tried to incorporate into my running life as well. You might be surprised to learn that despite the large number of races I participate in, and all the miles I log year after year, I do not adhere to any strict regimen or excessive training program. My training consists of two very fundamental principles: Log as many miles as possible while avoiding injury, and incorporate tempo bursts and hills into at least two runs per week. Other than that, there is no mystery to my training—no drills on the track, no soul-destroying hill repeats, and no obsession with lactic threshold and heart rate zones.

I discovered early on in my running career that the greatest threat to sabotaging a workout or missing a workout entirely more often than not comes from within. Let's be honest, there is always something that can get in the way of you getting out the door or heading to the gym. Modern life is an intricate dance of balancing work, family, and social schedules; and when push comes to shove, inevitably it's our commitment to exercise that falls by the wayside. A way to avoid succumbing to that daily internal dialogue of *Do I or don't I have time for my workout* is to eliminate the possibility for that question to enter your consciousness to begin with.

I exercise first thing in the morning, because I've found it the only time of the day when I can be absolutely sure nothing else will get in the way or demand my attention. On weekdays, the alarm wakes me up at 4:20 AM, and I quickly get dressed and head out the door for my run through the streets of Toronto. Before heading to bed each night, I check out what the weather forecast will be for my run so that I can lay out the proper running gear. You know what they say: "There's no bad weather, just bad clothing." I'm not going to lie to you; there are most definitely some nasty mornings in the dark cold of winter when my brain is racing with a million and one excuses for staying snuggled up in my warm comfy bed. Over the years, I can probably count the number of times on one hand that I've succumbed to that urge and stayed in bed, but on each of those occasions, I was racked with guilt the entire day for not going out on my run.

In the previous chapter, I discussed my aversion to running with an iPod or other music device, and my thinking there gets to the heart of my answer as to what goes through my mind when I'm running. I started running competitively about sixteen years ago, right around the time I entered a treatment program for alcohol addiction. At first, running merely provided a much-needed new outlet for me to get not only physically healthy but also mentally grounded. What I didn't know at the time was that running would evolve into a spiritual practice in my life. Running has been the only thing I've found that can quiet my mind and provide me the space and distance to process whatever life throws at me during the rest of the day.

Even though I don't have any music being piped directly into my ears via earbuds, that's not to say that I am not being constantly serenaded by the natural rhythms emanating from the streets, alleyways, and ravines of Toronto. The lack of traffic on my early-morning runs affords me the opportunity to run through the streets rather unencumbered by the increasing number of cars that clog our roadways for the better part of the day.

On my early-morning runs, I enter into an almost organic relationship with the pulse that underlies the breath of our city. I feel the vibrations of the streetcars grinding their way along the main arteries; I hear the faint echoes resonating through the narrow corridors of the downtown buildings as the trucks lower their steel ramps to make their predawn deliveries; and the nearer I get to the lake, the more I'm serenaded by the waves crashing into the breakwall or lapping up onto the shore.

Most important, because my mind is free of distraction and open to everything around and inside me, I'm intimately attuned to the cadences of the changing seasons—the playful screeches of the litters of baby raccoons in spring, the humidity-induced rumblings of the thunder off in the distance in the summer, the crinkly shuffling of the blowing and fallen leaves in the autumn, and the crisp crunch of the ice and snow underfoot in the darkness of winter.

Because running has grown to become the essence of who I am, no matter where I travel, it is always with me. When I close my eyes and think of all the places I've traveled to, my mind wanders back to the symphony of sounds of the battling car horns in Midtown Manhattan, the haunting wind whistling through the massive pines in northern France, the plaintive eagerness of the roosters' singsong in rural South Africa, and, most recently, the guttural mooing of cattle in pastoral England.

So returning to the question—*What goes through your mind when you're running?*—I would have to say the answer is itself another way of phrasing the question: *What doesn't go through my mind when I'm running?* For many of us, running has a way of bringing us back to the beginning. It recalibrates us. It silences us, and it calms us. The mere syncopation of our movement, combined with the opportunity for us to truly connect with ourselves through our breath, allows us to step back from the torment of that ever-present to-do list, and in the process find that place inside to simply *be.*

It is interesting to note that the psychological benefits of exercise in terms of an enhanced feeling of well-being are rarely felt during the exercise itself; rather, it's not until the return from this practice that we appreciate the space we cleared inside us. There is some kind of alchemy that takes place when we push our body outside of its physical comfort zone and enlist our muscles and aerobic system. After a prolonged hiatus from exercise, people often say things like, "I need to get back to the gym so I can burn off some of this stress" or "I'm looking forward to getting back at it so I can clear out some of the cobwebs in my head." And when you think about, isn't that what physical exertion is all about—the opportunity to grease the axle and keep our engine humming along?

Much has been written about the physical benefits of a sustained exercise regimen, and considering our society's obsession with body image and weight loss, that's not all that surprising. You may not even realize this, but for whatever reason you started running—to lose weight, to maintain a healthier lifestyle, or even to meet new people—the greatest benefit may be something far less tangible: a vast improvement to your overall mental health. Don't believe me? Take a look at any runner who has been forced to take some serious downtime as a result of an injury. I guarantee you'll find a squirrelly, irritable, and at times inconsolable athlete. So what's really going on there, and how is it possible that a reduction in physical exertion has such overt psychological manifestations?

Like so many of the runners I know, I initially took up running as means to manage stress—in my case, learning to live a life free of drugs and alcohol. The irony is not lost on me that in order for me to "reduce my stress" I gravitated to a sport that can take a significant physical toll on the body. I knew there must be easier and less expensive ways to alleviate stress, but I've found many of them to be lacking. So I hung on to running because even though I had no idea how it worked, it appeared to be doing so.

Throughout my sobriety, I've toyed with incorporating a meditation practice into my day, because the idyllic image of sitting serenely in the lotus position and getting in touch with my breath fills me with such hope. The reality is that meditation requires patience, something that, as anyone who knows me would agree, is definitely in short supply in my life. Having said that, there is no denying that once adopted as a part of your lifestyle, meditation can be among the most liberating experiences you will ever find. Meditation is freeing in that it has nothing to do with bringing anything into your life, and everything to do with learning to sit with whatever thought passes through you.

By helping to silence all the white noise around and inside us, meditation in its purest form is a process of *being brought to our own attention.* The challenge lies in learning to be comfortable coming face-to-face with those toxic stowaways that lie within us: the self-criticism, doubts, and fears that have an invisible hand in all that we do. The rewards for cultivating this focused attention and abstract awareness are the joy, empathy, and compassion that begin to displace the stress we carry within us.

Moreover, the leading researchers in the field of neuroscience have made significant discoveries as of late that point out how meditation can, for lack of a better word, rewire the brain. For the first time in the history of modern psychology, there appears to be hope that the impacts of embedded trauma and neuroses can be significantly curtailed, if not completely eliminated. According to researcher Eileen Luders, of the Department of Neurology at the University of California–Los Angeles School of Medicine, "Scientists used to believe that the brain reaches its peak in adulthood and doesn't change—until it starts to decrease in late adulthood. Today we know that everything we do, and every experience we have, actually changes the brain." From a layperson's perspective, this is not a huge leap in logic, as we can witness firsthand how malleable our brain actually is. Living through traumatic events such as rape, war, or natural disaster can have a recurring impact on a survivor's life, as it appears as though the trauma has been encoded into an individual's thinking process. We can also see how adaptive the brain is in that, like a muscle, it can be incredibly resilient when called upon to learn a new skill or be put through the rigors of intense academic preparation.

Like any aptitude, meditation is something we get better at the more we do it. It's said, "Neurons that fire together, wire together." I first became interested in the field of neuroplasticity when I started working with a therapist who was helping me process some physical and sexual abuse that I had experienced in my childhood. It is believed that exposure to trauma can have a long and far-reaching impact because when an individual experiences a traumatic event, his or her brain intervenes and cordons off different pathways in an attempt to isolate and lessen the effects. As a result of the psychological fracture, survivors of trauma often describe their lives as being pre-trauma and post-trauma. It's as if one life dies, and another commences.

In the field of psychology, an international team of researchers including Charles B. Nemeroff and Leonard M. Miller has discovered that "victims of emotional mistreatment were found to have a reduction of the thickness of the cerebral cortex in specific areas associated with self-awareness, self-evaluation and emotional regulation." It is believed that this part of the brain becomes desensitized as the brain enlists a protective mechanism to shield the individual from further psychological trauma. That all sounds great, but this brain rewiring, which served a positive function at the time of the trauma, continues to be a mitigating and to a large degree problematic factor in an individual's decision making and social interactions throughout the remainder of life.

Armed with this newfound knowledge that meditation may be the key to unlocking my feelings of being stuck in the trauma of my past, I once again returned to meditation as a way to rewire my brain out of this mess. But it's said, "Wherever you go, there you are." No matter how much I willed myself to embrace meditation, I continued to find no joy in having to sit still for any extended period of time.

It turns out, not all was lost. In my investigation into meditation, I discovered a branch of meditation that appeared to be right up my alley; hell, even the name appealed to me—*moving meditation*. Maybe the benefits of learning how to quiet my mind were not solely contingent upon my entering a Zen-like state, nor would I have to sequester myself in a dimly lit room as I stilled my body in a lotus position.

What is moving meditation anyway? In theory, it sounds simple: All that is required is your complete focus on whatever activity you are engaged in at the moment. Still, putting this into practice is another matter entirely. Let's not forget that we live in a society that not only breeds but also rewards multitasking. Breaking free from that natural inclination to overcomplicate the uncomplicated is much harder than it seems. Historically, moving meditation involved methodically walking a sacred path like a labyrinth or repetitively circumnavigating a large field or inner courtyard—the only guidance being that the individual empty his or her mind of everything but the sensation of the body moving in the moment.

From early on in my sobriety, running has been my faithful companion in both good and challenging times. And throughout those years, running has taken many forms in my life—in the turbulent times, as an escape or a respite; in more joyful periods, as a place of communion and, more recently, a spiritual practice in which my sanctuary is the deserted predawn city streets or the serene oasis of a backwoods trail. Therefore, the concept that running may be a way to pursue moving meditation was something I could wrap my head around. And for all I know, I have been practicing this type of meditation for years without even being aware of it.

In no way am I suggesting that you attempt to incorporate meditation in all or even a majority of your runs. Life has a way of getting in the way, so there will be plenty of occasions when your monkey brain is rightly preoccupied with the trivial and important tasks of work, family, and social priorities. Based on my own experience, I am all too familiar with how prone I am to zoning out on most of my runs. It's the time my brain prefers to wander as it unpacks whatever concerns weigh heavily on my mind, most probably because it's the only time my brain has to crunch away unencumbered on tasks that have preoccupied me throughout much of my day. Moreover, this is a special time in which I am most likely able to access my creativity and problem-solving skills.

Having hopefully sold you on the possibility of incorporating moving meditation into some of your runs, now is probably a good time to explain how you might put this into practice. It all begins with honing a keen awareness as you become attuned to all the sensations at play in and around you. Start by focusing on the physical sensations coming into you rather than on the mental observations coming from you. Heighten your sense of touch as you begin to feel how your body is an energy that moves through the space of the moment. Feel the subtle undulations as the ground meets your feet. With each foot strike, envision the kinetic energy or your feet moving in unison with the earth. Focus on body unity rather than on isolated physiometrics; in so doing, you extend the lens of your focus even more broadly. For instance, I pretend as though, like a horse, I am running with blinders on, so all I can see is what I am passing by or moving through in any given moment—trees, utility poles, and even other runners slide quickly into and then back out of the frame.

Instead of focusing on one area of your body, begin to connect with your entire body—feel the cold, the heat, and the moisture coming from your body and passing through the fibers of your clothing. You'll notice that your focus has shifted from the strain and tension held within your muscles, toward the sensation of touch upon your skin.

Once you have grown comfortable in this altered perception with this physical dimension of your running, it's time to become attuned to your auditory receptors as you begin to connect with the sounds around you. But here is the tricky part: Turn yourself over to this kaleidoscope of sounds and allow them to simply pass through your consciousness, but do not latch onto any of them. By that I mean, try not to obsess over the noise of traffic off in the distance, or the pattering of the rain as it splashes at your feet; instead, begin to view the sounds as just one more element of the terrain you are running through.

Before you move on to the more challenging part of the practice, I suggest that you spend at least a few months focusing on just these first two aspects of a running meditation—the holistic movement of your body through the space of the moment and the acceptance of the varied sounds around you. When you begin to feel more comfortable with the reorientation of these outward aspects of a moving meditation, then it's time to look at the more organic elements—the flow of your breath and the emptying of your thoughts.

As runners, we have a relatively easy time grasping the idea of connecting with our breath: No matter if you're a speed demon or long-distance plodder, your body has already intuitively landed upon its most efficient exchange of oxygen flow in the process of your countless hours spent running. Unlike the more common seated or lying-down meditation with which we are most familiar, moving meditation is less about moderating our breathing and more concerned with observing the flow of oxygen through our respiratory system.

Though the majority of our runs may feature a lot of gasping and panting, upon entering into this moving meditative state, we attempt to nurture the idea of following our breath rather than fighting our breath. As you become better at this practice, you will learn to check-in with your breath throughout your run. In so doing, you use it as a barometer that gives insight into where you might be holding tension in our body and what thoughts you are harboring that are unduly weighing on you and literally preventing you from taking a deep breath. Just as you allow the muscles in your legs to carry you up a steep ascent, follow your breath as it responds to the demands of your body's movement from moment to moment.

The final piece of the puzzle is the most challenging in its utter simplicity. I'd like you to picture yourself lazily sitting on a recliner on the warm white sand of a tranquil exotic beach. You are aware of the sound of the crashing tide onto the shore and of its retreat back out to sea, but at no time are you fixated on any one sound. Instead the sounds flow through you and back like the free-flowing tide itself. As you sit by the sea, your eyes gaze up at the clouds passing across the brilliant azure sky. One of these clouds may capture your attention momentarily, but as soon as it comes into view, another quickly takes its place. This is how it is suggested we allow our mind to flow within a moving meditation. When you are running, rather than trying to empty your mind, instead allow whatever thought enters to come in—and just as quickly leave again. Don't latch onto to any of these thought images, and try not to chase them.

If you do find that your mind is wandering, and believe me it will wander, then simply bring your attention back to the present and to your body's movement through this moment. Learning to follow your breath is the best way to cultivate this openness of consciousness, and just as many practitioners do in seated meditation, you may want to incorporate a silent mantra into your running meditation. Whenever I feel that my mind is escaping me and wandering, I enlist my go-to mantra: "Gentleness." As the cool air passes into my lungs, I fill my mind with the first part of the word, "gentle," and as the warm air escapes my lungs and passes through my nose, the second part of the word, "ness," enters my consciousness. The rhythmic pattern of *gentle–ness, gentle–ness, gentle–ness*, mimics the undulations of my feet pushing off from the ground, and my body moving through the fluctuating terrain.

The art of a running meditation is found in our ability to stay present within the moment and to see ourselves in communion with, rather than separate from the space we are running through. When it comes to articulating the beauty found in this meditative practice of living in the present moment, Eckhart Tolle's description in *The Power of Now* is second to none. "Beyond the beauty of external forms, there is more here: something that cannot be named, something ineffable, some deep, inner, holy essence. Whenever and wherever there is beauty, this inner essence shines through somehow. It only reveals itself to you when you are present."

Many of you may be thinking that in comparison with a more conventional form of meditation, a running meditation is somewhat of a cop-out—an easier, softer way. I have to disagree. Next to a seated meditation, a running meditation requires an even greater degree of concentration as you try to distance your focus from the physical pain, the burn of the lactic acid buildup in your legs, and the challenge of your footfalls on the uneven terrain. And let's not forget that the foundation of any meditation practice is predicated on one thing, and one thing only—carving out part of your day when you can fix your attention and reconnect with the flow of energy that runs through you. Meditation is a commitment you make with yourself; it's prioritizing your mental wellness by entering into a conversation or communion with you, and only you. Given the personal commitment it involves, I can think of no better sport than running to bring us to this place of inner peace.

The benefit of cultivating a moving meditation is contingent upon your ability to transfer this deep connection you've made with yourself to other facets of your life, and to take this heightened awareness with you long after your run has come to an end. The surest way to carry this feeling with you throughout your day is by way of gratitude. Acknowledge the beautiful dichotomy of running at its deepest form—that by making a commitment to *lose your self on the run,* you invariably open up a sacred pathway to *run into your self.*

In the words of the Vietnamese Zen Buddhist monk Thich Nhat Hanh, "Each step brings you back to the present moment; each step enables you to touch what is beautiful, what is true. And in this way, after a few weeks of practice, joy will become possible . . . Your love for the other, your ability to love another person, depends on your ability to love yourself. If you are not able to take care of yourself, how could you accept another person and how could you love him or her?" The goal of any meditation practice is not to eliminate thoughts from your mind or escape negative emotions, but rather the ability through awareness to lessen the dominion of those thoughts on your overall energy and well-being. In a sense, you are nurturing an ability to get unstuck from physical, psychological, and emotional trauma.

But most of all, come to acknowledge how beneficial incorporating the practice of moving meditation can be for your overall performance in the sport of running. The principles practiced in this meditative journey are those that we runners desperately need to incorporate throughout an endurance event like a marathon, or if we wish to have any longevity in this sport.

Running as Archeology

Hardship often prepares an ordinary person *for an extraordinary destiny.* —C. S. Lewis

From the playful Road Runner tattoo emblazoned on my calf right down to the rich oxygenated blood that pumps through my veins, everything in my being is a testament to the fact that first and foremost, I self-identify as a runner. Running has brought so many changes to my life, but none greater than bringing me to the understanding that life has little to do with striving for goals and chasing after dreams, and everything to do with scraping up against boundaries of discomfort and—with a little faith and a lot of patience—discerning how to navigate those delicate spaces.

When it comes to holding up a mirror to ourselves—and I'm not talking here about a superficial glance, but rather making an honest appraisal of what really sits in our heart and weighs on our soul—most of us shudder with fear at even the thought of what cowers there in the shadows. We spend a great deal of our life contemplating, and at times articulating, what inspires us, those magical things that make us tick. But within this process of self-appraisal, what often falls by the wayside are the less attractive elements of fear, mistrust, and pain—those feelings we spend a lifetime sidestepping and ignoring.

Rather than tear off the Band-Aid and dig into these wounds, we turn the lens away from us and look to external circumstances as the cause of our discomfort. In so doing, we enter into a vicious cycle in which we are constantly running away from the uneasiness that grows within, only to turn the corner and, at some later date, come face-to-face with that ugliness again, and again.

If the goal of psychological exploration is to rattle our cage and shine a light on those shadowy places, I would have to say that the sport of running serves as an ideal medium to awaken all that we harbor inside—the virtuous, the distasteful, and the neglected. I've witnessed this in my own life, as for many years running was my escape from everything that haunted me. But somewhere along the way I arrived at a place where I began to run toward, or should I say into, myself.

I feel so strongly about running's ability to shake things loose inside us that I've begun to think of archaeology as the perfect metaphor for running. The Society for American Archaeology makes an important distinction that "unlike history, which relies primarily upon written records and documents to interpret great lives and events, archaeology allows us to delve far back into the time before written languages existed . . . [It] can inform us about the lives of individuals, families, and communities that might otherwise remain invisible."

And to me, that's what running does for anyone who trusts in its ability to awaken a hunger inside us in our search for truth for something I believe to be among the most noble of human quests—our attempt to give words to that which "might otherwise remain invisible."

It's an all-too-common feeling that many of us feel stuck at various points of our lives because we see our personal past relegated to the annals of history—a radioactive relic or ill-begotten vestige locked in stasis. But in so doing, we deprive ourselves of any opportunity to work through or in some way come to terms with whatever it might be from our past that simply does not sit right with us in our present. We try to console ourselves by saying, "The past is the past, and best leave it there, just move on." Perhaps, this is a natural by-product of our Western view of linear time, but as anyone who has ever felt stuck, alienated, or alone will attest, there is most certainly residue from our past that lingers and disrupts our present well-being.

At times, it may feel as though your entire life is an house of cards built on a subterranean fault line. The emotional instability leaves you filled with trepidation as you gaze toward an uncertain future. It's been said that art is nothing more than reduction—the transcendent scraping away of veneers, the unmasking of the pillars of truth and beauty. In light of that, I would submit that running, in its purest form, is the fluidity of art in motion. I might even go as far as to suggest that a life given over to running is the purest form of reduction and self-reflection.

There is so much cruelty in this world, but the deflation and negativity we inflict upon ourselves may be the harshest of all. As the previous chapter pointed out, when you allow yourself to be truly present in your run, you have no other choice than to acknowledge what sits inside you, what joy lies in your heart, and what weighs heavy on your soul. The more faith you have in embracing this openness, the greater opportunity you have to run toward what scares you most. Time and again running reminds us that by surrendering to this vulnerability, we begin to arrive at our truth, as we learn to navigate the joys, the anguish, and the trapdoors of our personal landscape.

To push our physical and mental limits to their extreme, running asks that we divest attention and energy from the trivial preoccupations and frustrations of our day. By enlisting all our focus on the physical demands of the task at hand, we unwittingly quiet our mind to the point at which we can discover what lies buried inside us. Granted, this unearthing process may appear terrifying at first glance, but it's not long before we discover that there is no need to feel nervous in this undertaking: Unlike the probing experience of working with a therapist or psychiatrist, through the enlightenment of running, it is you who are doing the excavation or revealing of self. You end up feeling held and ultimately supported by the freedom that comes with learning to sit with, rather than be ensnared by, your past.

Running can be a remarkable catalyst for change in a person's life in terms of fitness and overall well-being, but what we often fail to acknowledge is its inherent ability to dislodge emotions and memories that have long since been entrenched in the recesses of the psyche. As John J. Ratey points out in his national bestseller, *Spark: The Revolutionary New Science of Exercise and the Brain*, whenever we engage in a high-intensity workout (75 to 90 percent of our maximum heart rate), our body responds to the perceived threat by slipping into a heightened sense of urgency. Part of this response involves entering an anaerobic state in which the brain releases HGH; this in turn contributes to an increase in our overall metabolic rate. If we push just beyond this upper exertion level for even a short interval, we are flooded with a sense of euphoria, more commonly referred to as the runner's high. Ratey indicates that this euphoric state is more than likely attributable "to the mixture of neurotransmitters pumping through your system at this intensity. It's the brain's way of blocking everything else so you can push through the pain to make the kill" (page 257).

Among individuals who report experiencing this exercise-induced emotional phenomenon, or runner's high, one thing appears to be fairly consistent—this feeling arrives from deep within, and more often than not comes on without warning. How this feeling manifests can run the gamut from an overwhelming sense of joy to a feeling of invisibility, or even to uncontrollable tears.

So where exactly are all these emotions and the subsequent disparate reactions coming from, and is it reasonable to assume that the body stores trauma and past experiences somewhere deep in our mind and muscles? Although scientific investigation into this theory is still in its early stages, I don't think it's far-fetched to assume that like a journal in which we record our thoughts at the end of each day, our body is itself a record of all that it has experienced—a record etched in laughter, tears, and sorrow.

Runners, by and large, engage in a very intimate relationship with their bodies, and as a result they are intricately attuned to every nuance or perceived change. Anyone who has ever had a deep-tissue massage is aware of how our muscles contort and hang on to the vestiges of stress. Practitioners of ART (Active Release Therapy) press, scrape, and contort the body in such a way that, lying on a table, a patient can experience the feeling of emptying or release of tension trapped in muscle and fascia tissue.

If we pursue this line of thinking, we start to realize that stress can be described as a physical and psychological manifestation of unprocessed emotions. And not dissimilar to the manner in which our immune system responds to the threat of a foreign intruder, our body and mind isolate the interloper (in this case psychological pain or trauma) and shield us from the perceived threat of unprocessed emotions. Taken to an extreme, the brain can, in effect, fracture and repress an acute traumatic experience to such an extent that the individual is unable to access the buried memory.

Mark Hyman, the American physician and best-selling author of numerous books on nutrition, describes it this way: "Your biography is your biology manifested as your biochemistry, and exercise definitely affects your biochemistry." If we approach it from that perspective, not only is our body a depiction of our entire life, but we can also take what we find there and use it as a road map to travel back into our past experiences. In a sense, we are afforded the opportunity to replay the film back through the landscape of memories, trauma, and lifestyle.

We need only look to the field of psychotherapy to find some startling new theories and insights into the connections between repressed or unreleased emotions, and their effects on our body and mind. One of the leading voices in this research is Dr. Candace Pert, a pharmacologist and professor at Georgetown University. Adhering to a holistic approach to the mind–body connection, Pert suggests that the mind and body are connected through intricate "emotion pathways" composed of chains of amino acids, known as peptides and receptors. These peptides are found throughout the entire body, and most notably in the hippocampus—the limbic system of the brain, and what is thought to be the key to unlocking our emotions. Pert believes that memories are not just stored in the brain, but are in fact encoded in the receptors throughout the body.

So many of the pivotal moments in our life, either joyous or painful, are associated with a life-altering or traumatic event. I know from my own experience as a survivor of sexual assault that I appear to have held on to the memory of that traumatic experience not only in my mind but also deep within my body. When something triggers my recall of the rape, a recurring series of events typically unfolds; as my brain spins and tries to make sense of the residual memory, my entire body stiffens, and I feel a hollow ache in my lower back and in the pit of my stomach.

This experience appears to give credence to the theory proposed by Dr. Pert and others in the field of psychotherapy, that even though we may be able to express, and in effect release, emotions stored in our brain, an emotion is not truly expressed until we are able to coax the entire experience of a past event out of the receptors throughout the body in which it has been encoded. In the words of Candace Pert: "Unexpressed emotion is in process of traveling up the neural access. By traveling, I mean coming from the periphery, up the spinal cord, up into the brain. When emotion moves up, it can be expressed. It takes a certain amount of energy from our bodies to keep the emotion unexpressed. There are inhibitory chemicals and impulses that function to keep the emotion and information down. I think unexpressed emotions are literally lodged lower in the body" ("Approaching a Theory of Emotion: An Interview with Candace Pert, PhD," by Lynn Grodzki, May 1995).

For whatever reason, conscious or unconscious, there are memories and emotions harbored within us that lie unexpressed. As Pert suggests, it requires a significant amount of our physical and mental energy to keep these emotions bottled up. Moreover, it's hard not to think that these stuck points don't play a role in our overall well-being. Some would even go as far as to say that all of this repressed energy is literally making us sick, causing undue stress on our immune system and leaving us prone to serious illness. By taking the entire body into account in the processing and release of emotions and memories, we appear to be moving away from the hyper-specialization of our Western medical model and moving toward a more holistic approach, one more aligned with Eastern medical philosophies, where the body is seen to comprise chakras and energy centers.

Whenever we are confronted with a painful or uncomfortable experience, event, or interaction, we commonly respond in one of four ways: First, we push back in hostility or visceral action. Second, we opt to suppress the feeling, and this often leads to heightened anxiety or depression. Next, we may attempt to subvert the experience with avoidance techniques or numbing—most often by turning to food, drugs, or sex—but ultimately this avoidance leads to further complications. And finally, and by far the response most conducive to promoting long-term physical and mental health, we can process and release this feeling through open communication, reflection, or physical expression. It's here in this final response that I see running, and other forms of physical exertion, as the key to unlocking our repressed memories and emotions, and thereby bringing us an overall improvement in our mental and physical health.

When it comes to repressed feelings and emotions, those born of trauma are by far the most tenacious and enmeshed. Before delving into an explanation of how running has helped bring me on a kind of archaeological dig through my own repressed memories and emotions, I thought it might be beneficial to step back and examine how trauma manifests in general.

By definition, trauma is a jarring event or experience that results in tremendous stress on our psyche, with ramifications so intense that our mind enlists various coping mechanisms to shield us from acknowledging or revisiting the painful incident. In the case of severe trauma, our brain fractures and walls off the unprocessed painful memory. This subtle shift in the brain's architecture can be most pronounced when the trauma occurs in childhood, a critical point at which the brain is in its most pliable and vulnerable stage of development.

Living with unprocessed trauma can be like continually walking through a minefield, as lurking around every corner is a trigger that has the potential to unleash further suffering and disquiet. At its most acute, trauma can distort our mental processing and outlook. We appear powerless as it leaches its way into all facets of our life and disrupts our sleep, appetite, and immune system.

Where trauma is at its most insidious is in the mysterious way it can confound, sabotage, and destroy our relationships with those who are closest to us. I guess that's why I've always considered the trauma I experienced as being like a cluster bomb: I have unwittingly allowed it to ripple out and collide into many of the relationships I have formed over the years.

Left unprocessed, trauma embeds in us and creates the conditions inside us in which we begin to inhabit a world of lies—those we tell ourselves in a vain attempt to dismiss or negate the significance of the trauma, and those we tell others to hide or insulate us from our shame. I find it helpful to think of trauma as energy—in this case, a form of negative energy that, left unprocessed, becomes internalized and enmeshed in every fiber of our body.

When we consider the outward manifestations of trauma, we see the immense toll it can take on a person's physical energy and its ability to cycle someone into depression. As I mentioned above, repressing painful memories and trauma demands a great deal of our physical and mental reserves, but it's important to point out that choosing to acknowledge and face those feelings head-on can be just as physically draining. In fact, our ability to revisit and process recessed trauma demands that we nurture a level of resilience and adaptive energy that allows us to function with the increased stress and dissonance that comes with unpacking the trauma and dismantling the facade and lies we've built around it.

When we look at the more sinister forms of trauma, those brought on by torture or abuse, we acknowledge that such events contain an added element of depriving a person of his or her willpower or control, and thus the trauma is further exacerbated. In this case, we can assume that the surest way to rebuild a life after trauma is to reinstill feelings of control and self-worth.

In order to arrive at this place of healing, it's important to first address the destructive coping mechanisms that the individual has enlisted to mask, avoid, or bury the trauma. This is why most trauma care specialists ask that their patients work on resolving symptomatic behaviors such as addiction and anger issues, prior to beginning therapy for the underlying issue of trauma. In my case, I spent over twenty years with psychiatrists, psychologists, and therapists simply putting out fires, but never getting to the heart of the problem.

It makes no difference whether you're an elite long-distance runner out for your scheduled two-hour intense workout, or a recreational runner simply looking to quiet your mind while you're out on a run. As we can see in the following account from Lauren, for many of us, running has the power to not only clear our minds but also shake something loose inside that may have been rattling around for years.

CIGARETTES, TRAIN STATIONS, AND AIRPORTS
LAUREN'S STORY

Author's note: In preparing for this book, I had the opportunity to interview many runners and ask them to articulate the importance of running, and the special place it occupies in their lives.

I've never been a runner. I'm still not a runner. I had just moved to Canada, I was alone; I had nowhere to go and wouldn't know how to get there if I did. I was twenty-five years old and had suddenly begun remembering the abuse I suffered as a child, at the hands of my father. Memories repressed for a quarter of a century came at me from every direction, fiercely and unpredictably.

I said to myself, *Am I crazy?* Suddenly it all makes sense. There's no way this really happened to me. Google says "repressed memories" were an '80s trend. My anxiety attacks started to last for hours, and I knew I needed help. So I did what any American would do: I called a doctor, told him I could pay today, and that I needed an appointment right away. I didn't understand OHIP (Ontario Health Insurance Plan). I didn't know it was illegal for a psychiatrist to accept money for a same-day appointment and a prescription for sedatives. I should have been skeptical about the cash-only deal, but I figured it was tax evasion and not medical fraud. Paying a premium for faster access to care is the norm in the US, not a red flag.

I left the psychiatrist's office feeling dirty, creepy-crawly, wrong . . . I filled my prescription and went home with what seemed like an answer. I stared at the bottle and my thoughts started turning dark. I became afraid of what would happen if I stayed still, so I did the opposite—I ran.

It was October, and it was unseasonably warm for Toronto, but I didn't know that yet because I'd just moved here three weeks ago. I ran through Mount Pleasant Cemetery, and then got lost in the winding cul-de-sacs of Rosedale and Summerhill, but I didn't slow down.

I remember as I child, I had to run "the mile" in school. It was humiliating because I was slow and chubby, and uncoordinated. I hated everything about it, and I hate the memory now. I've run through airports and train stations in countries around the world. But before that day, I had never really, truly, for no obvious and immediate purpose, just run.

That night, the night of my visit to the psychiatrist, after abandoning the bottle of sedatives, after smoking the last of my cigarettes, I ran. I ran faster than someone like me should—someone who lives a sedentary life, smokes, and maintains a steady diet of chips, salsa, hummus, and pita bread with the occasional bowl of cottage cheese. Oh, and a glass of wine each night. And by glass, I mean glasses, sometimes a bottle.

I "came to" at Yonge-Dundas Square, in downtown Toronto.

Being new to the city, it was the only landmark I recognized. I recalled thinking it was like Times Square, but not. And there I was under the glaring lights of the billboards, looking around and realizing where I was. I now know this is dissociation and a symptom of PTSD. At the time, I was confused, but chalked it up to a sober blackout . . . at least that's what I've always called them.

I wasn't wearing running shoes; I don't own any. I had no water. I ran as fast and as hard as I could and recall getting dizzy and disoriented but pushing myself harder, running faster. I was running from everything that had been chasing me, with every bit of strength and courage I could access. I reached Yonge-Dundas, snapped to, and physically felt a release of weight, emotion, and trauma. I started to crumble, but caught myself on a newspaper box. No one seemed to notice me, and I was grateful. And that was it. As if nothing at all had happened, I just started walking home.

Six kilometers is nothing to marathon runners—well, to most "runners" for that matter. I think it took me over an hour to walk home, knees buckling, hands shaking, sweating, and eyes blurred. I know how long it took me to run six kilometers . . . twenty-five years. And that night, for the first time in weeks, I slept without nightmares.

I CARRIED ON HOPING I WOULD
WAKE UP FROM MY DREAM
IRENE'S STORY

Author's note: Of all my interviews, the following account by Irene, from South Africa, might be the best example of running's cathartic effect. I'll let Irene's emotional words speak for themselves.

I want to tell you about my life after losing my husband two years ago. I'd been married for thirty years, and running for over twenty-three years. I had a very supportive hubby when it came to my sport; he joined the running club and ran for about eleven years, but he eventually gave up running. On the May 1, shortly after I had run the Wally Haywood Marathon, he passed away, suffering a major heart attack. I couldn't handle it. It felt like a part of me died with him, and a part of me blocked what happened to me. So, I carried on for seven months hoping that I would wake up from my dream. I didn't visit family and friends, and I never went out. I just stayed indoors by myself.

One day, some of my running friends came and dragged me along to do a race, and believe me, it was hard finishing the race! I ran into the finish with my head down knowing my husband would not be there, and my eyes searching for that special someone, and as I took the corner, the athletes who knew what I was going through all screamed my name and ran to the finish line, and hugged me and cried with me.

And after that, I found that I wasn't ready to face it all, so I got back in my shell. Later that same year after Christmas, I decided to go on holiday, and that's when something amazing happened. I went for a 10K race on the beach, 5K out and back. When I turned back for the second half, I looked at the sea and took my running shoes off and went in, and I sat down. You wouldn't believe all these small colorful fish that surrounded me.

I looked at all that beauty, and I realized the beauty of life. God had sent me there at that time, and I could feel that some healing took place. When I got back home, I registered for all the upcoming races and just started running. And I believe with the support of my fellow runners, it helped my healing. Even though I didn't finish the

Comrades Marathon in 2012, I returned the following year and finished in memory of my husband. Later, I placed my finisher's medal on his tombstone.

AN EGOMANIAC
WITH AN INFERIORITY COMPLEX
THE AUTHOR'S STORY

When I finally sobered up in my mid-thirties, my only motivation was not to die. What I wasn't expecting was the opportunity sobriety afforded me to welcome the world of running into my life. And this gift of running has allowed me to pursue what I now call an endurance lifestyle. It's as though each step I take as a runner nurtures more resilience in me, thus allowing me to come to a place where I can dig a little deeper into the negativity and twisted self-talk that causes so much disruption in my life.

What I am only just starting to realize is that all this time I've been building resilience has made me appreciate a critical life lesson: Setbacks may slow you down, but they are not to be feared! Running is an ideal metaphor for life because it reminds us that like the terrain under our feet, life is constantly shifting, and failure to take this into account can be devastating.

Like every runner, I've had my share of setbacks in the form of injury, poor race results, and the inevitable limitations of my physical biology. That being said, a little more than two years ago, anyone looking at my life from a distance would have seen a successful, happy, middle-aged man.

By this point, I had been clean and sober for over fifteen years, and I had all the advantages that come along with that—a wife and son who love and trust me, the kind of steady job that comes with being deemed responsible, and a long list of athletic accomplishments including having run over a hundred marathons and ultramarathons around the world.

But what wasn't visible from that vantage point was a man who was lost and alone. A man who had spent most of his life carrying around a secret in his soul, one so enmeshed in shame that it was eating him alive. In all honesty, I was closer to picking up that first drink or drug than I had been the day I sobered up all those years ago.

I had arrived at the most pivotal moment of my life—one steeped in fear, apprehension, and self-doubt. I now realize that if we are willing to sit with the discomfort long enough, uncertainty can be our greatest teacher; it reminds us that we in fact do not have all the answers. It leaves us open to new possibility and new directions we might otherwise have ignored. It all comes down to having the faith in yourself to let go of the reins so that you can quiet your mind and gain perspective.

I'm not really certain what precipitated the conversation I had with my wife; I think it was probably a coalescing of a number of images and memories that I could no longer keep buried inside me. It was early spring when I sat down with Mary-Anne and finally told her that I had been sexually abused by a hockey coach when I was nine, and it wasn't until a few months later, that I was able bring up a much more violent sexual assault that occurred when I was twelve.

As those fragile words left my lips, I could feel a rush of oxygen enter my lungs, and swear it felt like I had taken my first deep breath in years. I stared at the ground for quite some time, and tears poured down my cheeks. When I eventually got up the courage to take my gaze away from the ground and look up at Mary-Anne, I realized that she had been holding on to me the entire time I was speaking.

Despite what I had believed for years, in releasing that secret, my world did not come crumbling down before me. There was not a trace of pity or disgust in Mary-Anne's eyes—all I could see was love. I don't think Mary-Anne had any idea what she should do next, but it turns out, she did exactly what she was supposed to. It's only since I started reading more about trauma and working through childhood sexual abuse that I have begun to understand how difficult it is to really listen to someone. By trying to anticipate what someone else is going to say, we block any possibility of hearing what is coming from that person's heart and soul.

I had lived with the shame of sexual abuse for thirty-five years, and I permitted what happened to me as a child to define me as an adult. But once I'd decided to disclose the secret I'd been harboring, two important truths quickly became apparent. The first was that shame can only thrive in secrecy. The moment you decide to shine a light on your shame, it begins to lose the self-loathing it feeds on; it no longer metastasizes. What also became glaringly apparent was that sharing my story involves an intimate dialogue and, more important, finding people who are compassionate listeners.

At that time, we had been married for twenty-six years, and I'd always credited our open communication for the longevity of our marriage. That being said, only in the past two years, as we have been working through the disclosure process together, have I begun to understand that what most of us are looking for when we share our vulnerabilities and fears with someone else is for that person to be there *with* us—not be there *for* us. Whenever we see someone we care about in pain, our default reaction is to actively offer advice, to try to fix things or make something better. Well meaning as that may be, some things can't be fixed; instead, they simply need to be acknowledged and sat with.

Later that same week, I went for my intake meeting at the Gatehouse, a place that specializes in working with adult survivors of child sex abuse. I should probably add that I sat in my car in the parking lot for over an hour before I finally got up the courage to walk up the front steps into the building. Sitting in that car, I saw only two choices lying before me: drive away knowing that sooner or later what festered inside me would lead to my committing suicide, or walk through the doors of this building and be prepared to get more honest with myself than I had ever been before.

I sat down with an intake counselor and did what I'd never been able to do before, not even with my wife: I gave a detailed graphic account of what had happened to me as a child. And again, my world did not come crashing down at my feet. The counselor arranged for me to begin my treatment program when the next group started up, in about three weeks.

On the drive home from the Gatehouse that afternoon, I felt bruised and battered, and all I wanted to do was to wind back the clock to before I had let this secret out. Everything inside me was screaming at me to do what I had always done—just run away.

And that's exactly what I did. For the next three weeks, I avoided talking about it. I avoided everything that reminded me of my family and my childhood. I wasn't able to do much, but I was able to run, so that's what I did. I ran a lot! It was the middle of April, and the only thing on my calendar before I entered the treatment program was the Boston Marathon.

As fate would have, Mary-Anne had arranged to fly down with me to Boston this year. I had run it on many occasions, but Mary-Anne had only come with me once before. As our plane taxied down the runway and prepared for takeoff, I couldn't help but feel that, at least for the weekend, I was leaving all my problems behind in Toronto. Little did I know that this couldn't have been farther from the truth. Within a mere seventy-two hours, what I feared most was about to happen—my world would come crashing down.

Marathon weekend unfolded just like it always does. I went to the expo, visited with lots of friends, and ate lots of carbs. The first sign that things were not going as planned didn't arrive until the morning of the marathon. Boston had always been a weekend of celebration for me, a time to reward myself for suffering through the long, cold winter training runs. I'm usually joking around and relaxed as we board the shuttle bus out to the start line in Hopkinton. But on this morning, my stomach was in knots, and I couldn't seem to settle my nerves.

Not long into the race, I was overwhelmed with emotions, and the tears started to stream down my face. I tried to keep it together, but I quickly became a slobbering, snotty mess. The more I pushed through the emotions, the harder it was for me to catch my breath, and before I knew it I was hyperventilating and bent over at the side of the road. Somehow I managed to drag on to the halfway point of the race, but that's when one of the medical personnel saw me in distress and escorted me into the medical tent. I could see my chance of finishing the race slipping away, and to this day I'm not really sure how I did it, but I managed to convince the medical staff to let me back on the course assuring them that I was physically fine, just an emotional mess.

At around the four-hour mark, I crossed the finish line. By that point, I didn't care that it was my worst Boston showing by far. All I wanted to do was to fall into my wife's arms and to hear her say, *Everything is going to be okay.* I met Mary-Anne at the designated family reunion area, and for the first time I can remember, she wasn't able to conceal her concern for me. She had stood by me for all these years and steadfastly nursed me through my addiction, my depression, and my darkest days when I was suicidal, but here we were standing together, alone in a crowd in downtown Boston, neither of us having any clue how we would get through this together.

We headed directly back to the hotel, and while Mary-Anne went to the front desk to check us out, I jumped into the shower. A few minutes later, we were back out on the street headed to grab a quick bite to eat before our flight back to Toronto. We had only been on the street for a few minutes when we heard the deafening thud of the first explosion, quickly followed by a huge plume of smoke and a second explosion. It was absolute pandemonium on the street. No one knew which way to run, and the fact that most of the side streets near the finish line had been cordoned off for the marathon only seemed to add to the panic of the crowd. There's no need for me to get into detail; I'm sure you've seen the news footage and can imagine what it must have been like to be there.

We eventually made our way to the subway and headed to Logan Airport. We sat on the train in stunned silence among a sea of runners and their families, all of us in shock. We got to the airport only to discover that it had been locked down and all flights had been grounded. In the initial few hours after the bombing, the Boston authorities had jammed cell networks, so we weren't able to send or receive any messages. Everyone huddled around the televisions in the terminal, transfixed, as we watched the events unfold on CNN.

They allowed flights out of the airport a few hours later. We didn't get back to our house in Toronto until close to midnight. We crawled into bed, feeling completely shattered, but having absolutely no idea how traumatized we were by the events of the day.

I was due back to work the following morning at my job as an English teacher with one of the school boards in Toronto. At nine o'clock, I walked into the classroom, turned around, and faced the thirty-five students looking up at me. I opened my mouth to speak, but nothing came out. I ran out of the classroom and into the staff room to grab my jacket. I left the school and headed straight to my doctor's office.

Everything felt like it had all come to a boil, and I couldn't keep a lid on it anymore. I took a four-month medical leave from my job to get some help for the PTSD. I had absolutely zero attention span. I couldn't read or watch TV. I could barely have a coherent conversation. It was as though I was living a waking dream, as my world had come grinding to a halt while everyone else just kept moving on.

I filled my days by doing the only two things I could do. I went for a two-hour run every morning, and the rest of the day I sat in the green plastic Adirondack chair on our front porch and, like Jimmy Stewart in *Rear Window*, watched the intricate tableau of people's lives carry on right at the foot of our garden.

I think when your life feels like it's falling apart before your eyes, your greatest salvation, and perhaps your only recourse, is to fill your days with as much routine as possible. When I look back on this time now, I'm ever so grateful for the fact that next to Mary-Anne, running was the only constant in my life; and thankfully, I'd reached a level in my commitment to the sport where I no longer had to will myself to get out the door each day for my run. Running had become as automatic as brushing my teeth.

While I was off on my medical leave dealing with the PTSD, my weeks comprised regular check-ins with my doctor, gut-wrenching sessions with my trauma therapist, and tear-filled encounters with the men's support group at the Gatehouse Treatment Centre.

But this is why I believe that without a doubt, running has been my salvation. The more disengaged I became from my mind, the more in tune I became with my body. My mind had become a hostile disingenuous place, a landscape fraught with nightmares, flashbacks, and terror. Time spent there meant losing time. Hours would slip away from me as I sat on our front deck staring blankly out at the street.

I remember crying in my therapist's office as I searched for the words to describe what it felt like to watch my mind growing weaker—every day, that much farther out of my reach. Each session, she reassured me that when it comes to severe trauma, our brain responds best when it is allowed to completely power down in order to find the space and time to heal.

My body had become a perfect canvas depicting the contradictions that defined me. Here I was utterly confused, a forty-seven-year-old man with the robust body of a twenty-five-year-old, and the timidity and intellect of a nine-year-old. My only sanctuary in all this was found on a run. It was my church, my place of safety. It was the time in my day when I could completely shut off my mind and simply exist. Over the years, running had delivered me from the hells of addiction and suicidal depression. I had discovered that by gaining physical strength, there was a corresponding spike in my perception of self-worth and in my mental acuity. Running had never failed me before, so now more than ever, I was clinging to it like a drowning man to a life preserver.

Every night I drove home from the Gatehouse feeling lost and frightened, but I knew it wasn't hopeless. I'd been in the bowels of depression before, and I knew that what I felt right now in no way resembled depression. I was fragile, and fractured, but I could see all the pieces I needed to feel whole again, lying right in front of me. I just needed to figure out how to put them back together—rebuild some semblance of a life of joy.

There was a period when I cried and cried on every run I went out on. I had spent so much of my life bottling up all that emotion, feeling disgusted and ashamed about everything inside me, but now I didn't fight back the tears. They flowed freely, and it was as if the tears brought the clarity I needed to reclaim the part of me I had lost to sexual abuse.

I was no longer that nine-year-old boy running away in shame, or that addict turning away from his problems. With absolute conviction I believed that for the first time in over thirty-five years, I was finally running back to myself. Running had given me the space I needed to face those inner demons, and in that space I discovered myself. I was beginning to realize that through my running, I had become a type of cartographer, mapping out my inner landscape, a world in which I swam through my dreams and crawled through my fears.

So many of us are drawn to running for its ability to quiet all the confusion that surrounds us and infuses us. For me, it takes me to a place not of silence, but of stillness. When you're able to reach this place as a runner, it's not as though there is an absence of noise in your mind; rather, the fluidity of motion makes the space to hear whatever it is inside you that demands attention.

And how very ironic it is that I, and so many runners around the world, seek the solace of stillness in movement. Being surrounded by a tumultuous world that is in constant motion, I've grown to love running's capacity to bring stillness through the energy of release and the absence of concentration within the motion and the cadence of my body.

The journalist and novelist Pico Iyer summed this up so elo-quently when he said: "Anyone who has traveled knows that you're not really doing so in order to move around, but you're traveling in order to be moved." To me, that's the essence of running—its ability to move us through movement, taking us away in order to bring us back to ourselves. I have been fortunate in that through running, I have been able to find myself at many times in the middle of nowhere, literally and figuratively. But by being in the middle of nowhere, I believe that I am everywhere I need to be, if only for that moment. In running through trauma, I'm learning to trust less in my mind and more in my body, for it has taught me what to fear, what to love, and ultimately where to grow.

And just as my therapist had reassured me, ever so slowly my concentration and mental acuity began to improve throughout the summer and into the fall. The tears were still flowing on some of my morning runs, but the frequency with which I would have to pull over to the side of the road or trail in order to compose myself was definitely waning.

All the work I was doing with my therapist and with the counselors at the treatment center allowed me to return to those memories I'd insulated myself from for most of my life. I was fortunate to have the support of Mary-Anne to get me through the worst of the **PTSD** symptoms—the anxiety attacks that came on suddenly out of nowhere, and the almost daily night terrors that left me shaking in bed and lying in a cold sweat. I put my complete trust in my therapy team and in their assurance that the only way out of **PTSD** was to boldly walk through it. As soon as I thought I had arrived at a level of comfort with the trauma, it seemed as though another layer was peeled off and I was left face-to-face with another facet or embedded memory demanding my attention.

I had reached a critical point in my recovery in which it felt like I was sitting alone in the middle of a deserted room, surrounded by a disjointed mishmash of all my memories of the abuse from my childhood, scattered around me. Anytime throughout the day that I focused in on just one memory or image, I could feel my heart beating in my throat as the powerlessness began to overwhelm me. Looking back on this, I now believe that despite being surrounded by an incredible health care support team and a patient and loving partner, this was definitely the period of my life in which I felt the most isolated and alone. It rips your heart out knowing that you can no longer trust your mind to find its way to safety even though you see that path lying directly before you.

This was right around the time I discovered a book titled *When Things Fall Apart* by the American Buddhist nun Pema Chödrön. To my mind, there were only two responses to trauma that I would default to—avoidance: bury it, ignore it, avoid it; or actively trying every means possible to remediate it or fix it. I had reached the place where I felt everything joyful in my life was slipping away. I was doing what I had always done, but clearly it was no longer working. Reading through Pema's book, I was introduced to a third option—one that I'd never considered. Pema's words opened up the possibility for me to fearlessly inhabit that "room" I had created in my mind during the months of therapy, a room scattered with all the unearthed memories and images of a shattered childhood.

As Pema suggests, "We think that the point is to pass the test or overcome the problem, but the truth is that things don't really get solved. They come together and they fall apart. Then they come together again and fall apart again. It's just like that. The healing comes from letting there be room for all of this to happen: room for grief, for relief, for misery, for joy." And with that, I had found a solution, a tangible way out that really wasn't an escape after all. Instead of wasting all my energy trying to swim above or away from the trauma, I needed to get comfortable with its rawness by having it flow through me and around me. Time and again throughout my adolescent and adult life, I had brushed up against the ragged edge of adversity, the gnawing hollow ache inside, and each time I got too near the precipice, I pulled away or tried to soften its edges with drugs and alcohol.

I was awash in a newfound freedom, as I had begun to welcome a gentleness into my thinking precipitated by the Buddhist teaching that what we perceive to be an obstacle in our life is, in fact, neither good nor bad; it merely is. Running gave me the space and permission I needed each day to step away from self-judgment. Whenever a disturbing and jarring memory or thought came into my mind while I was out on my two-hour morning run, I would actively try to slow down my breath and repeat the following mantra: "I'm here. I'm well. Everything moves through me."

I know what you might be thinking: *This all sounds a little new-agey or airy-fairy.* But I assure you this simple reframing of my thinking caused an almost seismic shift in my ability and willingness to sit with the discomfort that was surfacing as a result of my trauma therapy. The most striking difference involved the issue of fear and how I could no longer ignore the fact that so many of my decisions were governed by the hold fear had over me. In my research on overcoming the effects of trauma, I came across a quote from the writer and inspirational speaker Karen Salmonsohn that really struck a chord. In coming to terms with a sexual assault in her past, Karen said she had to learn not to "fear change, but change fear."

Regardless of how much I'd journaled about fear, or how much I'd talked about it in my therapy sessions and 12-step meetings, I was never able to lessen its smothering and constricting effects, and that response ultimately relegated me to living a smaller and smaller life. In meetings of Alcoholics Anonymous, you often hear speakers refer to FEAR as an acronym for "False Evidence Appearing Real." As I mentioned previously, I believe that aside from the obvious health advantages of maintaining a regular running practice, within the space of running, we tap into a quieter place in our mind that allows us to digest, coalesce, and reflect on a vast array of emotions and ideas that, processed in their entirety or in communion, become less like an obstacle to be feared, and more like a teacher to be welcomed.

For six months after the Boston Marathon bombings, I was incapacitated because I had been trying in vain to battle PTSD simultaneously on two fronts: the sexual abuse from my past, and the more recent events of the Boston tragedy. Although it may sound counterintuitive, I was now convinced that the only way for me to break free of this trauma was not to get through it, but rather to run straight into it so that I could see trauma for what it really is—not toxic baggage to be lugged around, but beautifully misshapen pieces of life armor that, when woven together, forge a life of resilience, not one of fear.

But as spring rolled into summer, and then into autumn, I was slowly gaining a little more perspective on the events of the past year. I had been doing a lot of writing in my treatment program at the Gatehouse as a way to process some of the issues that had arisen in the group sessions. I'll admit it from the outset, I'm someone who thrives on structure, so I set out to complete thirty poems in thirty days, and I committed to posting each of them on Facebook.

The response I received from friends and family was incredible, and more important, as the issues came up during my treatment, the poems allowed others a window into the disclosure process and the lasting effects of sexual abuse over the course of a lifetime. In addition to the comments people were posting online, I started to receive private messages and emails from other survivors of sexual abuse and from their partners.

I noticed that the more I wrote about my past trauma, the less of a stranglehold it had around my life. What I thought would be a cataclysmic public explosion ending in further shame turned out to be a therapeutic unraveling and disengagement from that shame. Moreover, I knew firsthand that there were very few male survivors of sexual assault willing to talk openly about the impacts of that trauma on their lives, and I could see from the number of emails and messages that I was receiving that it was critical for me to step into this space and keep the dialogue going.

All of this was foremost in my mind when, in early September, I launched my blog *Breathe Through This* with only one governing principle: For the next year, I would write openly and honestly about the disclosure process—the joys, the heartaches, the still-unreleased shame, and, most important, the effects of this process on a marriage or partnership. The response to the blog was phenomenal, and within a few short months, I had reached over one hundred thousand readers. Fast-forward three years, and that "little" blog I started as a therapeutic process is now closing in on two million subscribers!

The messages began to flood in from around the world. People were relating to not only the issue of sexual violence, but also the overall message of resilience and vulnerability. With each article I published, I became more comfortable with the images and memories that had overshadowed so much of my adult life. I found inner strength and a belief in myself through my readers who recognized these qualities in me long before I ever did. Let me assure you that I in no way felt like I had a handle on this, but I was confident in my ability to wade knee-deep into the trauma that I had only begun to unearth.

I'm an early-morning runner, which can be both a blessing and curse. Believe it or not, when it comes to my running, I don't mind heading into the dark cold days of winter. I should come clean from the outset and say that I have a love–hate relationship with winter. My wife says I don't have an ounce of fat on my body, and that probably accounts for why I'm freezing from the end of the November right through until May. No matter what I do, or what I wear during the day, I'm always shivering, my fingertips are blue, and my feet are clammy. Having said that, when it comes to logging a three-hour run in bone-numbing windchill, I feel right in my element. I consider myself a hard-core runner, and I relish the fact that it's these nasty thankless training runs in the winter that build my resilience and allow me to dig deeper in the latter stages of the marathon than a lot of the other athletes I'm competing against who train on a treadmill to escape the winter cold.

Following the suggestion from my therapist, I decided to return to run the Boston Marathon the year after the bombings as a way to address some of the lingering issues of PTSD. This decision was based in part on a common practice in treating survivors of child sexual abuse in which, under the guidance of a therapist, the survivor is asked to compose a letter to the inner child. The process involves sitting down with a picture taken around the time of the abuse, and writing a letter to that child acknowledging how scared and alone the child feels, but also reassuring that he or she in a much better and safer place today. The theory being that through this letter, the survivor connects with a part of the past that had been fractured and walled off from his or her consciousness.

Believe me, I was skeptical about this process, as were all the other men in my therapy group, but that changed the following week when each of us stood up in front of the group and read our letter aloud while the other men passed around the picture of us taken as a child. At the end of that evening's session, there was not a dry eye in that room, and each of us was overwhelmed with the joy of having connected to a part of us that had been missing for so long. But that joy was ever so fleeting because in its wake was the bitter sadness of realizing how much of our lives had been governed by shame and self-loathing.

It has been two years since I sat down with my Mary-Anne and told her about what had happened in my childhood, and in the ensuing months, I've learned to put my faith in running as the means to carry me through some very dark moments that come with unearthing buried memories. I never thought I'd say this, but I wouldn't trade my life today for any other life. I wouldn't wish what I went through on anyone else, but having arrived safely on the other side,

I believe I am a stronger and better man for having gone through it. Am I fixed? Absolutely not! And if I'm to believe what Pema Chödrön has to say about that, there is no need to worry, because I'm exactly were I should be.

My experience, along with the stories shared by the other runners I interviewed during the course of writing this book, attests to running's exceptional ability to not only reveal but also assist us in processing embedded memories and the vestiges of trauma. If you're reading this now and struggling with something in your past that doesn't sit right with you, I invite you to explore how running may just be that outlet and release you've been looking for. The process is rather straightforward, and best of all, you can begin from wherever you are in your life.

The first step is to acknowledge the discomfort of this embedded memory or trauma, and to become open to the possibility that engaging your body in physical movement may unlock this discomfort. Next, be gentle with yourself and don't worry about setting a time line on this process or trying to take on more than you can handle. If recessed memories begin to surface while you're out on your run, see if you can locate precisely in your body where the memories have lain dormant. In Lauren's case, she felt an overall "release of weight and emotion," whereas with Irene, it was a vast emptiness that accompanied the tragic loss of her husband. For me, the trauma appeared to lie within the gnawing ache in my stomach.

By acknowledging where these buried memories have taken up residence inside us, we can start to appreciate how they have, in effect, taken on a life of their own. As you move farther into this process, the memories and trauma will no longer define you or govern your actions. The third step appears simple, yet it may be the most challenging for us. There is an incredible feeling of empowerment when we finally arrive at the place where we can label a disquieting emotion or repressed memory for exactly what it is. For Irene, it involved recognizing all the manifestations of grief that coincided with her husband's death. And for Lauren, unlocking memories of childhood trauma brought her to a better understanding of herself and delivered her to a place of strength. For me, I believe I was given the miracle of desperation—running permitted me the space I needed to finally understand that all my attempts to numb my emotions and bury my shame were destined to fail, just as they always had in the past. But the most transformational piece of the puzzle comes with the final step in the process of running as archaeology—recognizing that there is a great lesson to take from whatever memory or trauma you unearth.

When you start to acknowledge your body's ability to store and repress these toxic emotions and feelings, you gain valuable insight into what may be holding you back in life. The ultimate goal is to grow from the experience and foster a resilience that you can draw upon throughout your life.

It's All in Your Head

Nothing fuels a good flirtation,
Like Need and Anger and Desperation.
—Aimee Mann

The great German dramatist and poet Bertolt Brecht once said, "Great sport begins where good health ends." It's hard not to see the wisdom in that paradox, especially in light of our innate desire to brush up against the limits of human endurance. When it comes to the sport of running, it's not just world-class athletes in pursuit of Olympic glory who fail to navigate that fine line between a healthy pursuit and a perilous lifestyle. It's a sad reality that our sport is populated by runners willing to do whatever it takes to run farther and faster by testing the extreme limits of severe caloric deprivation, over-training, injury denial, and chronic sleep disruption.

There are those too who turn to running as their salvation, an oasis, a safe haven in which to heal, grieve, or simply sit with whatever adversity befalls them. When it comes to my own struggles with addiction, depression, and trauma in general, I've had periods of my life when I've relied on medication to get me through the day, and there have been times when that medication protocol was supplemented by my running practice. There have also been prolonged periods absent of medication, in which I relied on running as my sole form of therapy. I want to be perfectly clear that in no way am I suggesting that adhering to a regular exercise program can take the place of pharmacological treatment; in fact, my experience has dictated that this may not always be the case. That being said, we as a society appear to have reached the point where there is growing concern with our increasing dependence on prescribed quick fixes for our litany of physical and mental maladies. In a recent article in the *New York Times*, Dr. Richard A. Friedman, a professor of clinical psychiatry at Weill Cornell Medical College, spoke candidly about what he deems to be the limitations of the current generation of psychotropic drugs used to treat depression, bipolar disorder, and anxiety, and how psychotherapy has been shown to be as effective as medication in the treatment of common psychiatric illnesses such as depression and anxiety disorder ("Psychiatry's Identity Crisis," *New York Times Sunday Review,* July 19, 2015, page 5). In the words of Dr. Friedman, "There is often no substitute for the self-understanding that comes with therapy. Sure, as a psychiatrist, I can quell a patient's anxiety, improve mood and clear psychosis with the right medication. But there is no pill—and probably never will be—for any number of painful and disruptive emotional problems."

When it comes to embedded trauma such as post-traumatic stress disorder, patients respond best to treatments that elicit emotional responses or foster connections with others. In a sense, therapies such as CBT (cognitive-behavioral therapy) and CPT (cognitive processing therapy) assist patients in making the transition from "living in their mind" to "living in society." Further to this is the current discussion around addiction and how we go about treating addicts in society. In his Ted Talk titled "Everything You Think You Know About Addiction Is Wrong," Johann Hari makes the argument that our treatment model for addiction is heavily weighted toward punitive measures and isolation, or public shunning of the addict. Hari makes the argument that a lack of connection is what drives and feeds addiction in the first place. As Hari points out in his Ted Talk, we as a society tend to embrace a response to addiction like that seen in the popular television series *Intervention*. "Get an addict, all the people in their life, gather them together, confront them with what they're doing, and then say, if you don't shape up, we're going to cut you off. So what they do is they take the connection to the addict, and they threaten it, they make it contingent on the addict behaving the way they want . . . I began to see why that approach doesn't work, and I began to think that's almost like the importing of the logic of the Drug War into our private lives."

Taking all this into consideration, I'm led to believe that for many of us, running becomes that bridge to community, that ladder out of the void or darkness. My own experience living with an active drug and alcohol addiction is that there is no way around it, only through it—and that path is definitely messy, public, and humbling. The longer I've managed to stay sober, the better I've become at learning how to navigate all those times I feel disquieted in my own skin and how in those moments, I'm more inclined to push away and isolate myself.

Running has become such an integral part of my sobriety because it anchors me in a community of runners who have unconditionally accepted me, and see past my addiction to the me I'm trying to be. Being ensnared in an active addiction is a tortuous death spiral, an insatiable soul-sucking spiritual thirst, a cantankerous craving, a convoluted obsession that has little to do with seeking euphoria, and everything to do with self-negation.

As I mentioned previously, I turned to long-distance running early on in my sobriety as an escape from all the uneasy emotions that were bubbling to the surface. Today the greatest threat to my sobriety is that insidious drug known as complacency. While I'm quietly going about fashioning a life free of chemical dependence, that snake called addiction waits off in the shadows, slithering and seething, waiting for me to disconnect from all the love and support I have around me as I take those first steps toward the doorway of denial. Running has become the arena in which I combat my addictive mind's slide into complacency. I equate running with personal and community accountability, goal setting, and an overall commitment to better physical and mental well-being.

Over time, my connection to the running community has grown substantially, and I've noticed that as other runners get to know me a little better, they become more comfortable approaching me about the topic of addiction and my experience in recovery. The problem I'm faced with is: How do I even begin to describe what addiction is to someone who isn't an addict? In my mind, the closest anyone has ever come to capturing the self-destructive free fall into addiction is Dr. Vincent Felitti, who said: "It is hard to get enough of something that almost works."

I used to think my struggles with addiction were all about my craving to fill an insatiable void inside me. I'm only beginning to understand how mistaken that thinking was. Addiction has more to do with what I'm trying to avoid than it does with any void inside me. In fact, I no longer subscribe to the belief that, like the hole in a doughnut, we all have an empty space inside of us that desires to be filled. It's self-defeating going about your life thinking you're in some way broken, or that you're walking around with this aching cavern in your soul that incessantly screams out to be filled.

Time and again, running has shown me that I am indeed whole, that I am enough. The beauty of running is that there is only so much you can carry with you, literally and figuratively. This primal relationship with my running practice reminds me that life has given me limited space to work with, so if I want to welcome more joy, love, and forgiveness into my life, I'll need to make space by expelling some of the anger, hate, and self-pity that leave their fingerprints all over me.

For me, running is a not-too-subtle reminder of life's richness and fluctuation—prolonged periods of monotonous ambiguity, punctuated by moments of soul-crushing agony, and sprinkled with ephemeral euphoria. I disappeared into the world of drug and alcohol addiction because I was afraid—not of you, not even of something outside of me, but of the ache of the unknown inside of me. Running has given me the space to sit with that internal disquiet long enough to get to a place where I feel comfortable bringing it into the light. And the surest way to deflate or negate feelings of shame, isolation, or fear is to wrench them from the darkness. As I look back upon my journey with addiction, I'm reminded of the beautiful words of Naguib Mahfouz: "The problem is not that the truth is harsh but that the liberation from the ignorance is as painful as being born. Run after truth until you're breathless. Accept the pain involved in re-creating yourself afresh."

So if you're looking for me today, that's where you'll find me, running . . . running after my truth until I am breathless. I think this is an ideal time to turn over the remainder of this chapter to the stories of other runners who by the simple act of running one step at a time closer to their truth, have fearlessly faced some of life's greatest adversities.

WHATEVER YOU DO, DON'T LEAVE ME
MICHELLE'S STORY

I was with a guy for nine and a half years, and he was very verbally abusive. It came to a halt on Valentine's Day 2013. He assaulted me. He grabbed me by the throat and threw me to the ground. He was living with me at the time, so I threw him out of the house. It was my house, and has always been my house. I put all of his things in his vehicle, and from that point, it went from bad to worse—he was stalking and harassing me, constantly following me. It was a nightmare, so I started keeping a log of it.

Eventually, I went to the police. There were days I couldn't get out of bed to go out for my run. I went for an early-morning run three or four times a week, and he would follow me on those runs. I did continue all my physical activity. I had to. I told myself there's no way he's going to stop me running. He knew that running was my passion; I had started it just before I met him.

I was not an athletic child. In fact, I didn't start running until after I got divorced. My ex-husband found a new woman, and he told me the reason he found a new woman was that he didn't find me attractive anymore. I had put on weight. And that was twelve years ago. When I first started, I had the worst running shoes ever, and I couldn't even make it around the track. I don't know what it was that made me start running. I didn't have a bloody clue what I was doing, and I had the injuries to show for it. But I managed to eventually get around that track, and that motivated me to join a 10K running clinic at my local Running Room store. I met some great people there, and wound up running my first 10K and then a few half marathons with clinics. Even better, the weight just started to fall off, and going through a divorce, it gave me time and space to think. I remember saying to myself, *This is really great, why haven't I done this before?*

So that's where my running journey started, and this guy knew how important running was in my life. Once I kicked him out, the phone calls started—anywhere from three to fifteen times a day. I started thinking, *This guy is really losing it.* None of his messages and texts made sense, so I figured he'd gone back on drugs and started drinking again.

In late July of the same year, one of the guys he was working with approached me and told me that my ex was asking around where he could buy a nine-millimeter gun: "He says he is going to come up behind you when it's dark and take you down." He also said there was another threat, but he couldn't tell me about it because it was going to "freak you out too much." His advice for me was to go to the police immediately.

I rang the police, and they were here in ten to fifteen minutes. The police found him on a job site the following day. He was eventually caught after he had initially fled from the police. It turns out he was in the country illegally because he was on an alias passport. When he was picked up, they found him with two passports, so he was put into the Toronto West Detention Centre. He was charged with death threats, stalking, and harassment. He spent eight weeks in custody on an immigration bond. When he got out, he had to stay with his father, not far from where I was living.

During this time, I was under Witness Protection. I was assessed, and they put an alarm on the house and kept in touch with me. The police told me to change my schedule, and to stop running alone. I said to myself, I can still run alone—I bloody need this for my sanity. I had always run early in the morning around six, and a little later in the winter. There was no way I was going to let this guy stop me from what I was doing.

He was later deported back to the UK in November, and all the while, I continued running. The police had advised me to get out of town on the date he was released from the Detention Centre and again on the date of his deportation. On the morning of January 30 I left the house shortly before 7 AM and went for my usual run. It was pitch black, but thankfully for me it was twenty-one degrees below that morning, so I had on my balaclava and a hoodie. I was wrapped up nice and warm. I had only gone sixteen houses away from my house when two men approached me from behind. Luckily I had recently finished a self-defense class. All I can remember is one was strangling me while the other was going for my face. At the time I remember thinking, *They're trying to disfigure me.* They were battering me, so I yelled and fought with all my might, and when I eventually hit the ground, the guys ran away. I can remember hitting the ground and shouting, "You fucking bastards!" I pulled the phone out of my pocket because I had started running with a cell phone, and I called the police. I didn't think I had gotten ahold of them. I wasn't aware at this time that I had been stabbed. I made it back to the house, and called the police again. They stayed on the phone with me until help arrived. It wasn't until I was put onto the stretcher that I realized I had been stabbed because my sports bra had soaked up all the blood. I was slashed to the back of the neck, the cheek, the lip, and they narrowly missed my main artery at the collarbone.

They rushed me to a trauma clinic, and I was in the ICU for three days because my neck swelled up to thirty-six centimeters, so they were worried it was going to cut off my windpipe. They basically just stapled my neck, and fortunately I didn't need surgery. And the couple of blood clots cleared on their own as well. I stayed in the hospital for another three days, but when I was released, I was not allowed home for another week because the house was still a crime scene.

When I finally did come home, the police and Witness Protection came to see me. They wanted me out of the house, and they told me no more running alone—"You got to move." I told them I needed at least six months to think about this decision. At this point, I obviously wasn't running yet. The funny thing is, when I was in the trauma unit at the hospital, I knew I wasn't going to die, but I just kept thinking, *Shit, I'm paralyzed. I can't move. How the hell am I going to run if I can't move!*

When I eventually was released and I knew I was going to be able to run, my biggest concern was the fear—I was afraid of the dark. I was afraid of hoodies. I couldn't go into an underground parking lot. I was afraid of everything. I couldn't even put the garbage out.

Anyway . . . I decided not to sell the house. I had security cameras installed and bars put up on the windows and doors. I had the staples removed from my neck, but I felt pretty good—battered and bruised, but okay. I remember when I had the staples removed, I asked the doctor when I could run again, and I'm sure he felt I had kind of "lost the plot." He said, "At least three weeks, because you've got a lot of internal damage."

Sitting at home I said, *How the hell am I going to get out there and face this fear" I've got to run past that spot. I don't want to walk past it. I've got to run. I can't run in the dark anymore.* I knew I had to get back out there; otherwise, this guy had beaten me. He specifically had me attacked when I was running because he wanted to take that away from me. Whether he wanted to kill me or disfigure me, I will never know to this day. Fortunately, I'm a tough old bird, and I've healed really well.

So I Googled run clubs, and found the Toronto Run Club, and discovered they met Wednesday nights and Saturday mornings. I put on my running shoes, but I have no idea how I got out the door—

I was absolutely petrified. I did tell the group what had happened because I was so fearful of being left on my own while we were out on the group runs. It was only six weeks after the attack, and I was basically shitting myself, but I knew I had to get back out there. I needed to get my life back. And it felt great, but I didn't really connect with anyone in the group.

I met a girl in the group who asked if I wanted to join her on her Sunday-morning run, and believe me, I never ran on a Sunday morning because Saturday is my night out. I told her I was a bit slow because I'd recently had a setback, and she said, "Don't worry; run with me." She told me about a woman's run club that ran out of the Running Room on two mornings a week, and that's where I eventually met Lucia, the facilitator and coach of the women's clinic.

You know what? When people ask me about the attack, I always tell them, when bad things happen, something good always comes out. Since joining Lucia's group, I have met the most amazing women who will be friends for life. Running . . . well, I love it even more. I don't miss running alone even though I used to like how it cleared my head. But now, running is more about being social. It's fun. It's changed my life for the better. I'm so disciplined at work that I never would have left to skive off for a run in the middle of the morning. But now it's nice that I get a break in my day to go for a run with the ladies. I get to run in daylight. I've learned so much from Lucia and all the other women in the group. In fact, this year I've actually run half a dozen times on my own! I went for a run one morning at seven when it was light, and said to myself, "Fuck you. You bastard. You're not taking this away from me!"

I run past that spot all the time, and honestly, I feel so strong. I did ten weeks of therapy with a psychotherapist that was all covered under Witness Protection, and the police kept in touch with me throughout the process. They'd come by the house or just pop by—

they were amazing.

As I mentioned, I am starting to run alone, but I would never run in the dark. I think that's just stupidity. So many runners today are connected via social media, but I've had to be very careful about that. Lucia's group does have a private Facebook page, and I participate on that, but under a fake name. I don't have a picture on my profile, and I don't post anything on my own page.

I work from home, so I need to get outdoors during the day for some fresh air. I don't care if it's minus twenty-one. Get your clothes on and get out there. And now it's about being with other people as well. Without that, I don't know what I would do. I don't think I'm running away from anything. I think I'm running toward health, happiness, and feeling better, ready to take on the world.

If I were giving advice to someone coming through trauma, I would say you have two choices—you either go up, or you fall down. Keep going and enjoy what you're doing. You can't let that trauma take over your life. You've got to live every second to the fullest. When you come that close to death, and I was very lucky they just missed that main artery by a fraction of a millimeter, you have to live every day to the fullest. I appreciate things more—my health, all the small things in life that we just push to one side. My mom was just over to Canada for a visit and she said, "You know what . . . You have no mental scars. You make the most out of every day." I tell myself, *You don't know how lucky you are. You woke up this morning. You've got legs. You've got feet. Get out of bed, and don't complain about these stupid little things that don't matter anyway.*

People ask me, "Are you scared in the house?" You know what— I slept with a baseball bat in the bed with me for six months. It's not in the bed anymore. I have a panic button beside my bed for my alarm. I now can keep some of the windows in my house open, and I'm not scared anymore.

LEARNING TO FAIL BETTER NEXT TIME
ANTHONY'S STORY

I suppose with any good story, the best place to start is at the beginning. And note that I *do* consider this a good story. Without the terrible things that I went through nearly seven years ago now, I would not be where I am today, and I can tell you, there is no place I'd rather be right now. My life is happy, full of hope, promise, and love, and better than I ever could have imagined. Today I can stand unafraid and face the world, knowing that I will meet every challenge that comes my way with my head held high. I may fail in many of these, but I have learned not to fear failure anymore, but embrace it. And fail better next time.

But fear is where my story starts. For most of my life I have felt afraid—afraid of failing, afraid of not fitting in, afraid of being different. And I was different, but not so you would necessarily notice. I developed Tourette's syndrome in early childhood, and have suffered from it since. Now, I can say that I was fairly lucky, and any motor tics that I have had I have largely been able to hide from people around me, but it took its toll. It had a big part in shaping how I felt about myself, which in general was not good. I really can't complain about my childhood, and I made the best of it, but fast-forward a couple decades, and regardless of what I was or accomplished, I never felt happy with myself. Never quite good enough, never quite smart enough, and always hiding my Tourette's from the world.

Although I had that rumbling in some dark pit inside of me, outwardly my life was great. I had graduated from medical school, started working in a busy practice, was fairly successful, and had somehow miraculously found the most amazing woman in the world, whom I later married. So I had absolutely no reason to feel sad, or insecure, or down on myself. Yet I did. And then one day I took a pill.

Now, people are going to believe whatever they want to about addiction. Maybe they think it's a choice, maybe they understand it as a disease, or maybe it reflects a weak moral character. Regardless of what anybody thinks, I truly believe that addicts are wired differently from everyone else. They react differently when their body encounters that substance for the first time. The exact opposite of what you would think. The drugs or alcohol are not the problem. The brain instantly identifies them as the solution.

And so it was for me. After a fairly minor shoulder injury, someone handed me a Percocet and told me it would help my shoulder. Well it did. But more important, it helped everything else. I didn't feel unhappy anymore. My tics seemed noticeably less. I felt better, like everything was just perfect. Before I knew it, I was chewing eight pills at a time, several times a day. I knew instantly I had a problem, but I simply was too terrified, too helpless to do anything about it. So it continued, spiraling more and more out of control, until I was taking an inconceivable amount of pills per day just to feel normal, just to function.

It no longer made me feel good, but I needed to take the pills just to not feel sick. My life had become a nightmare that I was powerless to wake up from. I was scared, alone, and terrified that I would just wake up dead one morning, leaving everyone wondering what the hell happened. There were only two possible outcomes. I would die, or I would be found out, both sounding equally bad to me. I was found out.

My life came to a crashing halt, everything falling down around me. I was suspended from practicing medicine. I confessed every-thing to my wife who through some undeserved twist of fate sup-ported and still loved me. I then did the hardest thing I had ever done in my life to that point. Locked myself in my home and with-drew cold turkey. I spent the next five weeks in rehab. After a long drawn-out battle of over a year, my license was reinstated and I was allowed to get back to work, but not before my story was splashed across the front page of our local newspaper.

I don't know what it was, if it was just out of a sheer need to get back up, or to provide for my family, but I started to crawl out of the hole I was in. I got back to work. My patients welcomed me back with open arms. My family and my wife stayed by my side. I had come through this nightmare.

As I was just about to return to work, something happened. My wife challenged me to run a half marathon. Thought it would be good for me, she said. Something I could be proud of. She was proud of my recovery, but thought that maybe I could do this to get myself mentally and physically back together. Though I survived my ordeal, it had taken its toll, and I was a shadow of my former self. I had never been a runner before this. Although I had tried to run to keep in shape in the past, I didn't really like it. But my wife had chal-lenged me, so I figured maybe I could do a half marathon—maybe I could challenge myself, push those boundaries. So I ran.

In 2010, I completed my first half marathon. Got sick the day before and nearly pulled out, but I could not bear the look on my wife's face were I to tell her I might not run. Letting her down again. So I got myself to the start line, and made it across the finish. And I liked it. It was hard, but I was proud of myself. I could do some-thing that day that I couldn't before, so I started to run on and off after that, and started enjoying it more, pushing myself here and there.

Here is where the story may get a little goofy sounding, but bear with me, because this is where it all changed for me. At the end of 2012, I heard that they ran marathons through Disney World. I had always had a soft spot for all things Disney, and I thought here would be a real challenge. Travel down to Florida and run a half through the happiest place on earth. And in the first month of 2013, that's exactly what happened, and it changed my life forever. This is where I got the sense of the power, the magic, the vibe of what running was all about.

I still get chills when I think about toeing the line with tens of thousands of other people, running through the thick early-morning fog while monorails whisk silently above you, turning the corner and seeing the castle lit up in the early dawn sky just for you. I have never experienced anything so moving in my entire life. And I ran like a madman. It was my fastest race ever, and a sense of accomplishment overwhelmed me. This was me! I was a runner now.

I remember being in awe of an eighteen-year-old kid who ran the Goofy Challenge that year. The thought of running a half marathon back-to-back with a full marathon was absolutely insane to me, and knew that I could never do something like that, but then I remembered the quote from Walt Disney himself: "All our dreams can come true if we have the courage to pursue them." So when I got home, I signed up for my first full marathon that summer. The very next year, I returned to Disney to run the inaugural Dopey Challenge, 48.6 miles over four days, but not before doing back-to-back 10K runs and a half marathon on the other side of the country in Disneyland.

I was hooked you see. There were thousands of runners of all shapes and sizes, speeds, and abilities. I saw a place where no one judged one another, and where we all shared a common goal—to challenge ourselves. The guy next to me wasn't my competition, but my supporter. Strangers smiling, talking, thanking volunteers. A sense of camaraderie that was so pervasive that it was unspoken. This has been my experience at every race since. And every race is a new goal, not for anyone other than myself. I get to prove to myself each and every time I lace up that I can do something today that I couldn't yesterday. All of a sudden, I wasn't afraid. Failure was just another opportunity. Not finishing was not a failure; the only way I could let myself down was not starting.

I took this newfound confidence and energy and channeled it into my work, my family, and my life. I began lecturing to medical students, residents, and physicians about physician health and addiction. My patients saw my transformation, and it inspired some of them to try the same, and more important it pushed me to talk to my patients more frankly about what they could do for their health. The one thing that so many of us fail to invest in is our own health. The physiological benefits of exercise are far beyond any medication I can prescribe or any other treatment I can suggest, and that holds not just for physical ailments, but for mental health as well. It is no secret that exercise results in a boost of neurotransmitters that is more profound and sustained than that offered by antidepressants. And the side effects are awesome. So I opened up to my patients, encouraged them, took the time to talk about physical activity, and challenged them to push their activity.

My addiction nearly killed me, and I fought my way back to health, but not until I started running did I truly feel alive again. I'm proud of where I have come from and excited to see where I'm going. Life is an adventure, and I can live it to its fullest. Life still has not been all roses, and tragedy has befallen my family and me since I have recovered, but I can put to use what I have learned to face tragedy head-on, and get through it.

It's all right there. The will forcing you to hold on, filling each minute with sixty seconds' worth of distance run . . . everything I have been through is in there. I have gone through a terrible battle, but it has made me what I am today, and through running, I have experienced and seen and felt more than ever before, and truly tested my limits, and learned what it is to break through them. Whether I have a good day's run or a bad day's I run, it centers me, grounds me, and puts me at peace. My addiction does not define me, but it is a part of me. My running defines me—strong, resilient, hopeful, and above all, grateful.

THREE LIFELINES ON THE ROAD TO WELLNESS
JENNY'S STORY

When it comes to running, I guess I'd say I'm running away from my past life—a life filled with abuse, addiction, chaos, and mental illness—and I'm running toward sanity and stability. I suffer from Bipolar Type 1 disorder, and I've found that running stabilizes my moods and, along with medication, keeps me in remission. My bipolar did a 180 when I started training, and that was when I realized how important it is in my life. My relationship with running has rescued me in a way because it allows me to function in all other areas of my life. Three things are my lifelines—lithium, AA, and running.

I ran a little bit in university, but it was just on the treadmill, and then in my addiction, the only running I did was from the (imaginary) police. When I got sober, I was very sick physically and on and off meds for years. I finally stepped on a treadmill again when I was detoxing off a very strong anti-anxiety medication. I was just desperate to feel good, so those short little twenty-minute treadmill jogs probably saved me from using during that time.

A year and a half ago it was my brother who suggested I train with a team and a coach, and he helped pay for it. I am forever grateful because that changed everything. My bipolar finally went into remission. I now feel I'm tapping into a love and passion for a sport I never knew was possible. I can run six days a week and train at a high level, and all the while feel fantastic. The positive change in my mood and energy level has begun to spill out into other parts of my life; along with working at CAMH (Centre for Addiction and Mental Health), I'm applying for graduate school and writing my GREs. I think the running has given me the confidence that I wasn't getting in other areas of support in my life—like AA—and running has helped me to really conquer those things I've been so afraid of.

Many people may turn to running and other forms of exercise as a substitute for medication, but I think for more serious cases like mine, exercise acts as an augmenter to my medication. My psychiatrist told me that she would like me to be on twelve hundred milligrams of lithium; however, because I run, I am fine at nine hundred milligrams, and as far as I'm concerned, the less the better. Running could never completely replace medication for me because when I am in an episode, either manic or depressed, I am too crazy to even think about running. If I were in a manic episode, I might go out and run fifty kilometers at a blistering pace and destroy my body. I understand that in order to keep running, I need to take my meds. But for milder cases of depression or anxiety, I really do believe that regular exercise is a miracle drug. And to be perfectly honest, I would be a lot faster if I weren't on lithium, so this is something I struggle with a lot!

Overall, I'd have to say that my life has been a struggle—it's been about surviving. Running makes me live as if life's about *living*. When I got to kilometer 40 on my first marathon, I started to cry because

I knew I could do anything after that. Even without racing, running makes me feel strong. When shit hits the fan in life, I can always just put on some shoes and run it out.

THE FINE LINE BETWEEN A HEALTHY DISTRACTION AND COMPLETE AVOIDANCE
ANNIE'S STORY

I started running around 2008 when another personal trainer at the time said to me, "You really need to stop eating so many cookies." Little did she know I was submerged in an ongoing battle with an eating disorder (restriction, bingeing, and purging). I started running, but my relationship with running at that time was to run so very far away from everyone—including myself, and my eating disorder.

As a professional registered dietitian working daily with patients suffering from mental disease, both medicated and not medicated, I recognize that exercise does help them. But there is a very fine line between a healthy distraction and complete avoidance when it comes to dealing with an internal battle. So that's why I believe, like medication, exercise should be prescribed or recommended in doses. I've known many runners, including myself, who used it to get the endorphin high but never dealt with their issues. Ultimately, I believe it can supplement meds to some level, but for many, it's a part of treatment.

It took a few years for me to really figure out why I run. Despite being quite talented with a goal to hit the Olympic qualifier, I fell out of love with road racing because I only started doing it to show others I could be someone I'm not; perhaps to be ultrathin again. After some time off and reworking my goals with my current coach, I decided trail running is where my heart actually lies. I don't have to run for others, I can be me. I now don't run away. I run to be a professional. It's about personal gain now. It's taken me seven years to change my outlook on running, and there is so much more to it than just exercising, or being in shape.

My running practice started with an idea to do a half marathon—to strike it off my bucket list. But I ended up placing in that race, and thought there must be something here, so I raced, and raced, and raced. I was injured often, probably because I was naive and didn't know any better. But I was winning all over, going to Boston every year, and putting in so many miles. Little did I know it wouldn't last long. That high ended after two or three years, and injury left me depressed, angry, and on edge all the time. I started working with my current coach, and I've become smarter as a runner. Today I fuel and hydrate for my sport, not my eating disorder. I have set those thoughts aside and solely focus on being a better person and runner. People know me for my running, and although that adds pressure, it feels good. I am a runner and forever will be. I went from running and hating myself, to running and loving myself. A beautiful transformation!

WOULD MY CHILDREN EVER
BE ABLE TO FORGIVE ME?
SANDIE'S STORY

My relationship with becoming a runner became intentional when my second son was three months old, and I needed a way to wear off the accumulated baby fat. Running also gave me a break from being constantly needed by two young boys and a husband, something that felt suffocating at times. And without realizing it then, it gave me the sense of accomplishment that I was missing from taking time from my career. I didn't have a network of other moms around for support, and spent many afternoons in tears after feeling like I was just talking to the walls all day. I look back on that now, and think it was possibly depression that went unrecognized.

Not too many years later, I had to come to terms with the heartbreaking reality that I wasn't happy in my marriage. I knew deep inside that I wasn't the right parent to be the primary caregiver—my husband had taken over most of the nurturing and domestic duties while I was trying to play the role of primary breadwinner. I had allowed the role reversal to take place, thinking that it was the right path, but something about it was also very wrong. Deep down I knew my boys weren't getting the authentic version of me, and they deserved better than that.

Running became my therapy, and my form of self-flagellation for all of the guilt, shame, and pain of having to be a mom who leaves her sons. When the break finally happened, and I became the visiting parent, running was my solace. The pain of running faster and farther gave me relief from the pain I felt inside from missing not being able to tuck my children in at night and wondering whether they would ever forgive me. It gave me a way to grieve, to pray, to release the anguish and soothe the pain in my soul.

I clearly remember the run that changed everything. It was just another run on the treadmill at the gym—isolating myself from everything around me with a headset and loud, gut-wrenching music, as I pounded faster and faster for as long as I could. In that state, nobody approached me to chat—they likely could see I wasn't actually there, but deep inside myself working through my own personal hell.

It was my habit to take myself down as far as I could to find the depth of my pain, and then work myself back up to purge it so I could carry on with my day feeling some relief. That day, I made a plea to my guardian angel, or whoever was out there looking after me, for help. It came in the form of a new realization . . . that I could be doing this to become stronger for my boys instead of beating myself up. I had to be running toward something instead of running away. It changed everything.

I'm a believer in finding strength and healing through moving meditation, regardless of the form that it takes. My own running, then cycling, and now triathlon, gives me a channel for dialing into my own resources to find clarity, release, and purpose. This is the active part of my own therapy. Self-help books, writing, and talking with others is the passive work that helps to expose the work that needs to be done. Then it's time to get busy.

The worst experiences have given me the most opportunities for growth that, in turn, translate into life resilience. My first marathon ended with me losing control of my bowels and feeling humiliated and completely gutted. As I sat on a curb in Central Park shivering in a foil blanket and reeking in my own stench, I had to make a choice: sit there until someone comes along to help, and suffer further indignity of both circumstances and helplessness, or get up and carry on. I chose to get up, and to this day, I continue to get up whenever my life takes a shit all over me again and again. Looking back, I can laugh when I tell that story, but it taught me a lot about how important it is to take better care of myself, and that you can just carry on when life gets messy. Making the decision is the critical moment; after that, it's just work.

EVEN THOSE IN THE HELPING PROFESSIONS NEED A LITTLE SELF-CARE
KATE'S STORY

I would say that I'm definitely running toward my better self and happiness. When I was younger, I was super skinny, and a basketball coach said I was "too slow" to ever play in a game, so I was benched all season. I think I run partly to prove that she was wrong. No one is ever "too slow" to be a runner.

I began running about six years ago, and more recently turned to long-distance running. I started running with a group of co-workers as a way to relieve stress after a day of working at the Psychological Trauma Program at CAMH (Centre for Addiction and Mental Health) in Toronto. It was a way to disconnect from work and reconnect with each other.

I ran because I wanted to be present in the moment rather than overstimulated and stuck in eight billion thoughts. I've become a smarter runner and have also learned to enjoy running, rather than seeing it as a means to an end. I think running has taken me from someone who didn't feel that she was very athletic into someone with greater confidence in my athletic abilities and also someone whom other people would consider athletic.

Based on my personal and clinical experience, I believe that exercise works on the behavioral and social aspects of mental health that are not always addressed with medications alone. Mental health difficulties often lead to social isolation, a reduction in pleasant and productive activities, avoidance of triggers, and a decrease in general physical activity. As people no longer engage in pleasant and productive activities, they often feel worse, and this becomes a vicious cycle. Many psychotherapies (e.g. cognitive-behavioral therapy) focus on changing behaviors to change mood/anxiety by encouraging people to re-engage with life and to seek out the activities that helped them feel better in the past in order to feel better in the present and future. Exercise can change unhelpful behaviors by increasing physical activity and social interactions, decreasing avoidance, and giving people a sense of accomplishment and pleasure.

When it comes to running, I'm most definitely a tribe member. I have always run with a group as a way to socialize, process the good and bad things in life, and as a way to remain motivated. I have chosen to use running as my non-competitive, low-pressure activity, so the moment it stops being fun or becomes too competitive, I'm out. Running has forced me to push my limits and to realize that I'm stronger than I give myself credit for. For me, it's not just about physical resilience but also mental resilience. Long runs in particular test my mind more than my body. I have learned to bounce back from a bad day based on all of the times I've managed to survive and conquer bad runs.

A BROKEN HEART, A TUMOR, AND
THE LESSONS ALONG THE WAY
LISA'S STORY

I came to running in an attempt to get away from something. Two months before our wedding, my fiancé decided he no longer wanted to get married. I was devastated and felt so lost. I can't recall why, but a friend gave me a copy of *Runner's World* magazine, and it was the annual half-marathon issue. So then and there, I decided to train for my first half marathon. What I had initially thought would be the worst summer of my life was in some ways the best one. I loved to run—every time I laced up and headed out the door, the sad thoughts couldn't keep up with me. The pain of my breakup felt constant during my day-to-day, but it faded to the background once I was in motion. The race later that fall was exhilarating—I was hooked.

The year following my breakup, doctors discovered I had a sizable pituitary tumor affecting my entire body. I was very sick, but among the myriad problems was that my joints hurt so much I could barely walk, let alone run. After neurosurgery to remove the tumor, I was bed-bound for ten straight days, and you'd be amazed at how fast the body can atrophy. All I could do to keep my spirits up was to visualize myself out on the trails again one day, and I used that same visualization to get through all the MRIs and CT scans too. I closed my eyes and imagined myself bounding along the trails near my cottage.

Once released, I had to start with lots of walking, but eventually I got to run again. Sadly, it wasn't for long as the tumor's impact upon my body left other areas of damage, which also required surgery.

Three additional surgeries later, I was finally on the other side of my illness.

I'm well on the road to my comeback now. I see myself as neither running toward something nor away from something, but rather alongside something. It isn't so much about getting away from thoughts and feelings anymore, nor is about getting to the finish line, nor the race T-shirts and the hardware. It's about staying in motion to work through what's going on in my life. Be it stress or a perceived problem, or something troubling—well anything really—it's as if I now bring all of it along with me on the run. I keep what's bothering me alongside me for the run; quite possibly because I anticipate the new perspective that running always offers.

I'm much more balanced when it comes to my running now. There was a point when I was obsessed with my times and my distances. My Garmin once died during a run, and I actually almost stopped running because I thought: *Well, now this doesn't count.*

I think that the best thing everyone can do is to find his or her running, whatever that may be. It could be skiing, skating, or cycling; or perhaps it's yoga or Pilates. Whatever physical activity brings you joy, that should be a fundamental element of your treatment plan. Never underestimate the ability of sweat and exercise to cleanse the mind, body, and soul.

LIVING IN THE EYE OF A HURRICANE
REBECCA'S STORY

I began running in the eighth grade because a teacher saw potential in my abilities. At that time, I was still being sexually abused, but it had been going on long enough that it had become the norm. I was able at that point to interact fairly normally with my world and compartmentalize that portion of my life, at least as best as a thirteen-year-old can. I was quite good at running from the start, and it was something I loved, not just because I was good at it but because it provided the eye of the hurricane, if you will, in my life.

When I was in high school, however, I was a slave to running, and running was indeed a cruel mistress: My form was atrocious, and I didn't understand what physical limits were. Even back then, the little tastes of confidence and freedom running gave me were addicting. But most of all, running allowed me to control the pain to my body, as it allowed me to set limits and turn it on and off. Running did not damage my soul, and that was almost the complete opposite of my experiences with trauma and hiding it. These qualities led to overtraining to the extreme, so as a result, I ended nearly every track season in my teens with stress fractures. It's important to note as well that at this point, the effects of running were entirely limited to running—any sense of control or freedom only existed when I was running, and not when I was in school, or working, or at home.

When I started running, I was certainly running away from a number of things, as it became a refuge from shame, fear, and sadness. Running paralleled my insistence to not believe, admit, or process what had happened to me as a child, and it helped me to muffle the confusion, at least temporarily. I truly believe this was the case because when past trauma began to rear its ugly head in my life, and I was unable to control its effects on my thoughts, not surprisingly, I grew increasingly distant with running.

I barely competed during my senior year of college and during the six months following graduation. This lack of competition was not due to a lack of motivation associated with depression, or the fear of transition after college, but more because I had become disenchanted with running—It had ceased to provide the magic that it provided me before. I could no longer run away from things simply by running. When I started running again last March after a four-month complete hiatus, preceded by an eighteen-month period of disenchantment, I immediately noticed that running was still a refuge for me: It still provides a haven in solitude and a sense of tranquility. However, this time around it seemed as though I truly believed that I was a good runner, that I was a strong runner. I think it is a little early to be positive about this, but thus far I feel like I am truly running toward becoming that person whom other people perceive me to be. I am running toward confidence and self-worth, and without a doubt running allows me to process these conflicting beliefs and emotions that can otherwise be smothering.

I think people who have never run seriously think that running is a solitary endeavor, just as people who have never recovered from something difficult, like trauma, may believe recovery to be a journey you must take on your own. To an extent, they are right: Every distance runner at some point is going to have to put in a ninety-minute-plus run alone, in the extreme cold or heat, with nothing but himself or herself to rely on for motivation and strength. But the strength, the joy, and the camaraderie that come with a team, a running group, or whatever formal name describes your running tribe—well, that is an incredible thing. I can say firsthand that my teammates and I share a bond that is different from, but similar to, friendship. There's something special you have with people with whom you share physical pain and encouragement when they are at their physical "low points." You spend hours talking, even when there is limited blood flow to your brain and you are ten miles into a fifteen-miler. These bonds have been incredibly important both to my running as well as to my personal life.

In some of my hardest times, I asked my teammates to hold me accountable for things like going to class and showing up to practice.

They did this, no questions asked, and probably kept me from having to withdraw from school or get kicked off the team. I owe them a great deal, and there is an understanding among us that if one of us ever desperately needed help, the others would be on their way.

Had I not grown into an adult while running, I would be much less self-reflective, self-aware, and goal-oriented. I think that running has helped me to be what I need to be for myself and for others. This includes being present in the moment, professional when I need to be, and tough on myself when I need to be. I hope that as my practice continues to grow, it can help me become kinder and gentler to myself and to others.

A Resilience Boot Camp

Only to the extent that we expose ourselves over and over to annihilation can that which is indestructible be found in us.
—Pema Chödrön

In sitting down to write this book, and in conducting hundreds of interviews with runners from around the world, one core question kept coming up: Where does inner strength come from, and is it something we can foster? One of the consequences of being a high-profile endurance athlete has been that my own struggles with addiction and trauma have been somewhat public, and although many might construe that as being a huge downside, in fact it has been incredibly empowering: Through this open discourse, I have begun to understand the importance of resilience not only as a quality I want to nurture in my life but also as a catalyst to inspire others to face their own challenges.

One of my favorite quotes that epitomizes the tenacity and elasticity of this transformative quality comes from the American writer and pastor Joel Osteen: "We may get knocked down on the outside, but the key to living in victory is to learn how to get up on the inside." These words are a much-needed reminder that fortitude is brought to light from inside us, and may not immediately reflect what is happening around us.

I'm also attracted to the idea that victory is something we are "living in," rather than the sum total of our accomplishments or acclaim. I believe that somewhere within this subtle mind shift in how we perceive adversity lies the answer to where inner strength manifests and what we need to do to foster it. I would also suggest that resilience is not an endless stream that we can tap into whenever the need arises, but rather a precious reservoir that must be tended to and prudently nourished. When we speak of inner strength, I have no doubt that it is born of the return from adversity rather than from crags and gnashes of the journey itself.

I was listening to a Jonathan Fields interview with author and entrepreneur Nilofer Merchant on the *Good Life Project*, and she was asked how she managed to overcome the incredible hardship and trauma of her past to get to where she is today. Her response was quite enlightening: She believes there are two types of people in the world, and both are working from the same ledger. There are those who define themselves by the column of the ledger that tabulates all of the failures, hurt, and disappointment in their lives. And the second group consists of those who choose to define themselves by the column listing all the choices they've made to overcome each of those obstacles in their life. If you look at life like that, you start to see that resilience is not the absence of or immunity to setbacks and disappointments, but rather your ability to embrace the belief that even in the failure of the moment, you have enough faith in yourself to pick up the pieces and keep moving forward.

There are as many definitions of *success* as there are people on this planet, but when it comes to success, I'm reluctant to equate it with money, power, or prestige. Success for me is a by-product of having the tenacity that flows from an unbreakable spirit. Adversity is the greatest of equalizers—it makes no difference who you are, there will come a time in your life when the ache of loss or an over-whelming fear will shutter you, and quite possibly shatter you.

Having spent a great deal of my adult life wading through the wake of sexual violence, addiction, and prolonged periods of perilous mental health, I had begun believing what so many people around me were telling me, that maybe I am resilient, and that this is in effect the positive takeaway that comes from living a life touched by trauma. But as I began unpacking this perception a little further, I realized that something about it didn't quite sit right with me. In no way was I going to settle for simply being resilient. For sure, people who are resilient are inclined to pick themselves back up in the face of ad-versity. It's hard to argue that this is not a good thing, but to my mind, it really has very little to do with growth and moving forward.

I have to credit my wife with this change in my thinking. It was she who pointed out that in addition to resilience, I had resolve—that deep sense of inner purpose that keeps you bouncing back up and propels you to rise above whatever obstacle lies in front of you.

I know it's a delicate difference in semantics, but it is one that has the possibility of yielding immense personal growth. There is defi-nitely something to be said for soldiering on and rebounding from setback after setback. No doubt, it speaks volumes of your tenacity. The problem lies in where I and so many others get trapped—living in a vicious cycle of being knocked down and getting right back up again, so much so that it's hard not to feel like life's punching bag. And when it comes to runners, I think we are in some way pro-grammed to repeat this self-destructive cycle, as we are often immune to listening to the subtle messages of our body—ignoring repetitive injuries and falling into the same ineffective or stagnant race strategies time and again.

But how can we expect to ever break this cycle? I believe the an-swer is found in what we do in the midst of the adversity, this chaotic dissonance, and not in what happens once we have already re-bounded. There is no denying that we are a pain-averse society. We gravitate toward avoidance and numbing, rather than surrendering and enduring. I suggest the greatest opportunity for personal growth, and thus the possibility for substantive change not only in our running but also in our life in general, comes just after the moment we are naturally inclined to turn away from the discomfort. In so doing, we deny ourselves the opportunity to listen to the lesson that echoes within the discomfort. As William James said, "Most people never run far enough on their first wind to find out they've got a second."

Author Caroline Adams Miller sees the roots of this problem in how we raise our children—doing everything in our power to insulate them from challenge and failure. According to her, "This is not a gritty generation" because teachers and caregivers have become so consumed with building children's self esteem that most children lack the grit necessary to achieve long-term goals. But all is not lost; in a recent article in the *Washington Post,* Judy Holland states that the latest "research shows grit is usually unrelated or inversely related to talent. But if you fear your kids are light on grit, don't worry. We can cultivate traits of gritty people, and model them for our kids. Grit is contagious."

This brings us to the question of whether or not there is a blue-print for cultivating grit, and if so, are there steps you can take right now to build it within your life? This is definitely a question that comes up a lot whenever I give a talk on overcoming adversity, so I thought I would share a few of my adversity-fortifying strategies with you.

TREADING WATER WON'T
GET YOU TO THE SHORE

One of the greatest challenges as an endurance athlete is to strike that perfect balance between living in the moment and envisioning the broader picture, and for me, this involves laying the foundation upon which I can ensure that running will be my faithful companion long into the future. Whenever it feels as though all I'm doing is just going through the motions or barely managing to find the joy in running, I like to step back and reassess my priorities. Often it comes down to the simple question of what I am willing to give up in order to pursue the goal I am chasing. You'd be surprised by what this introspection can reveal in terms of the cost of your pursuit of running in regard to your health, your family, and your time.

As you move from recreational running, to 5K and 10Ks, to half marathons and marathons, and possibly into the world of ultramarathons, you will find yourself tumbling farther down the rabbit hole into the outer limits of our sport. And you'll start to grasp that the toll it takes on you physically is but one aspect of the cumulative stress running can have on your life.

Running, like anything worth doing in this world, demands that we make space for it in our life. No matter what their ability or their preferred distance, the one thing all runners can agree on is that there are increasing demands on our time, and as a result it's not very difficult to find a valid excuse not to run today. For many years, I felt as though I was balancing on a high wire attempting to keep all the balls in the air—my family, my job, my sobriety, and of course running. It's an unenviable position to be in because you're constantly weighing priorities and deciding what you're willing to sacrifice. It really was a fool's game because looking at that list, running appears on the surface to be the most expendable, and thus the one most likely to be tossed aside. As a result, I headed out the door on each run with a gnawing sense of unease in my stomach because I had decided to spend some me-time rather than time with my family or friends. Further complicating this was the fact I was out three or four nights a week at AA meetings in order to maintain my sobriety. It wasn't until about eight years ago that I began looking at the role running fills in my life from an entirely different perspective. Returning to the analogy of juggling balls on a high wire, I now understood that running was not one of the balls I was juggling, but was in fact the high wire itself. My commitment to running had become the one constant during my day that grounded me and allowed me to be more present in my interactions with family, work, and friends.

To say that this was a monumental shift in my thinking is a vast understatement. Running no longer was part of an either–or equation; it had become an inseparable part of my day—an activity that nourished me, cleansed me, and revitalized me. By acknowledging the power of running in this way, I silenced that debate that took place daily in my head about whether or not I would find time to get in my run. I had little doubt that running made me a better husband, father, and employee, but I was also keenly aware that left unchecked, the demands of running would leach into the time for me to be present in every other relationship in my life.

It all comes down to choices and deciding what you are willing to part with. I decided to reschedule my day to become an early-morning runner. When the alarm goes off at 4:20 AM, I avoid the trap of hitting the snooze button, and I jump right up and get ready to head out on my run. There are definitely a lot of advantages to being a morning runner—there is less traffic to contend with, the air feels fresher, but most of all, there is no chance that some schedule snafu will sabotage my run plans.

When our son was younger, my early-morning runs meant that I was home in plenty of time to help out with child care and family responsibilities, but even all these years later, I continue to adhere to my morning routine because it grounds me in a better disposition to face the day ahead. It certainly means going to bed earlier, but the way I look at it, I more than likely would be spending those late-evening hours in front of the television anyway.

THE JOY LIES IN THE PURSUIT

I've always been one of those people who find joy often lies in the pursuit rather than in the acquisition, so it's probably not all that surprising that I have become somewhat of an adversity junkie. Don't get me wrong, I love the feeling of crossing the finish line in a big race, setting a new PB, or looking down at the finisher's medal that was just placed around my neck, but those moments seem so fleeting compared with the euphoric glow I receive in the midst of a grueling workout or physically draining week in my training schedule.

That being said, there is a big temptation that in pushing the limits of your endurance and focusing on the adversity and challenge of running and training, you might begin to obsess over how difficult everything is—and before you know it, you have lost the joy in the sport, and every workout becomes just another thankless chore. It reminds me of a quote by the American poet Tyler Knott Gregson: "Promise me you will not spend so much time treading water and trying to keep your head above the waves that you forget, truly forget, how much you have always loved to swim."

So how does one go about pushing the limits of physical endurance, yet avoid the pitfalls of disenchantment that come with overtraining and the monotony of the daily training grind? To me, the solution to this running impasse is also the answer to many of life's most pressing problems; it lies in letting go of the illusion of control. I was recently listening to one of the last interviews the writer and educator Bruce Kramer gave before succumbing to his battle with ALS—although he'd probably refer to it more as a dance than a battle. In the interview, he was discussing how every one of us struggles with something that is beyond our control, and in fact, it's our humanness that naively convinces us we have control in the first place. What struck me the most was when Bruce said that in order to find that place of serenity, we have to find a way to "grow into the demands of that which is beyond us." I find these words so enlightening in that they remind me that learning to see the adversity of running as a challenge, as a gift in disguise, is not only a way to willingly lean in and embrace that adversity but also a gentle reminder that beauty is found amid the chaos on our way to attaining our goals—whether they are in running or in life in general.

MAYBE IT'S TIME TO GO TO YOUR BENCH

Though on first glance it may appear to be a solitary activity, running actually feeds on our connection to the people with whom we surround ourselves. One of the greatest assets runners can have to insulate themselves from adversity and inevitable setbacks is to amass a diverse and supportive resilience team. I've made little secret of the fact that I've struggled when it comes to having a close relationship with my family of origin, but on a positive note, this has compelled me to rethink what family means to me and to find ways to extend that definition to those people with whom align myself.

Even if you are fortunate enough to have nurturing family members around you who support your passion for running, I invite you to consider developing your own resilience team. These people most typically function in one of three roles: a buffer who shields you from being overwhelmed by self-doubt or debilitating adversity; a booster who rallies you and fills you with confidence and motivation; and a bumper who gently nudges you out of your comfort zone toward growth.

Ultimately, the people you choose to surround yourself with can be your lifeboat or parachute, but if you don't choose them wisely, all you're left with is a lead balloon or a leaky raft. There is most definitely overlap in these roles, and there will be times when you will naturally be inclined to embrace the boosters in your life, when in fact that's time when your trusted bumpers question whether you've set the bar high enough to step out of your comfort zone. Regardless of how strong you feel as a runner, it will be the people on your resilience team who will remind you of why you turned to running in the first place—a path you set out on to build a better, more resilient you.

THE SEEDS OF DEFEAT LIE WITHIN US, NOT OUTSIDE US

Having completed more than a hundred marathons to date, and probably three times that number over the course of my ultra training, I have an intimate understanding of what it feels like to dig deep when everything in your brain is screaming at you to quit. Tomorrow's disappointments are built on the bedrock of today's failure, so an important part of becoming resilient as a runner involves learning to recognize when you are unwittingly setting yourself up for inevitable failure. Most runners are familiar with the often touted advice of not increasing weekly mileage by more than 10 percent, not introducing anything new on race day, and not setting unreasonable time goals unsubstantiated by your base training.

But what I mean by "not setting yourself up for failure" goes far beyond those rather tried-and-true running taboos. Over the years, I've witnessed a lot of friends in the running community growing despondent with what feels at times to be the unrelenting grind of training; as a result, they fall out of love with running. If you track back to the root of that disenchantment, it invariably is related to their chasing an elusive dream of a prescribed time goal for which they are ill prepared.

I totally get where they are coming from, and as a someone who lives with an addict's brain every day of his life, I can tell you that the satisfaction of hitting that time goal will be quickly replaced by waning thoughts of how you might have shaved a few more minutes or even seconds off your finishing time. GPS watches that track every stride of our run, permanently archived online race results, and the competitiveness of social media postings have all managed to erode the essence of why most of us decided to lace up our running shoes in the first place. We might be wise to remember that resilience has a lot to do with longevity, and the surest way to sabotage any chance of being a lifelong runner comes the moment we sacrifice the joy of pursuing our passion for the vain pursuit of what comes down to rather meaningless time goals.

The richness of running for me lies in how it can sustain my overall well-being long after the run has ended. Time and again, I'm shown that a key component of resilience is adaptability, and a critical first step in building stronger bridges between your running practice and the rest of your life is becoming more aware that life has a way of interrupting your passion. Failure to take into account that sometimes you need to forfeit your run or deviate from your training schedule because of unforeseen scheduling conflicts, family commitments, and even weather anomalies can leave you feeling dejected, emotionally frustrated, and physically depleted—none of which is conducive to building resilience in your life.

Over the course of researching and writing this book, I had the pleasure to interview hundreds of runners from around the world, and in my conversations and emails with the running community, one theme kept popping up—the belief that 90 percent of the success we attain from running does not occur on the road or on the trail, but between our ears.

There's no denying that we are our own worst critics, and that often manifests in a self-defeating mantra of believing that what happened before will inevitably happen again. One bad race or even a string of subpar training runs does not doom you to failure. Instead, take the opportunity to look on those days as touchstone moments of potential growth and reevaluation, a barometer to measure your run–life balance. Whenever I encounter a tough patch in a training cycle or feel overwhelmed in a long race, I make sure to remind myself that by quitting now, I make it that much easier to give up on myself the next time I face adversity, be it on a run or, for that matter, in any facet of my life. Patterns are easy to establish, and once they're become entrenched, it's very difficult to break them.

It was Robert Frost who said, "The best way out is always through." None of us likes to sit with pain or suffering, but by learning to be present with it and listening to the lessons it whispers to us, we begin to see suffering not as an obstacle in our path, but as a stepping-stone to growth and transformation. When it comes to choosing between grit and natural talent, I'd chose grit any day of the week. To me, nothing is more inspiring than witnessing the tenacity and elasticity of grit honed in the trenches of resilience.

Every year at the end of December, I look back over my log of the year's runs and reflect on the runs and races in which I've excelled and on the points at which I struggled. I find this such a cathartic and enlightening practice because it reminds me of two inescapable facts about running: First, with age come slower times and slower recovery from injury; and second, the runs that resonate most with me are those where I had to dig deepest to fight through fatigue, battle the weather, or—as is most often the case—wrestle with the demons inside me. Running has become my landscape—the stage on which I play out my life one step at a time.

Most important, running has shown me that adversity is not a destructive force, but rather something to be at peace with: Within its dissonance, we discover the strength and beauty that was waiting to be born inside us. When I finally sought the professional help I needed to address my drug and alcohol addiction, the obvious benefits to my physical health followed in short order. However, my early years of sobriety were punctuated by extremely tenuous mental health, as I continued debating with myself about whether sobriety meant I was recovered or recovering.

Running is to be cherished because it reminds us that by walking into something that frightens or disarms us, we permit ourselves the opportunity to learn from adversity. And as the biblical story of Jacob teaches us, if we are to find the truth hidden within our struggle, we ought to face our adversity and exclaim: "I will not let thee go, unless thou bless me" (Genesis 32:26).

While researching this book, I put a call out on social media inviting runners to email me their own stories of how nurturing a running practice has made them more resilient overall in their lives. The response was heartfelt and overwhelming, so I thought I would share a few of those stories with you now.

THE HEART OF DARKNESS
RHONDA-MARIE'S STORY

Author's note: Rhonda-Marie Avery is the founder of The Envisions Project, a nonprofit organization aimed at empowering other-abled athletes to achieve their own adventures. The Envisions mission statement says that the organization "seeks to create awareness for 'other'-abled athletes, and through this, we hope to create a space for discussions of how to incorporate inclusiveness into everyday ideas of sport. Envisions believes that disability and sport are not often intertwined in our society. If you see them together at all, it's marginal. Disabled athletes are out there, taking part, trying hard, and competing. There are many groups and organizations that offer support networks to disabled athletes, but finding and connecting with them can be a struggle. Envisions is here to take on the task of bridging the gap between accessibility and adaptability." In August 2014, Rhonda-Marie, an endurance athlete who just happens to be legally blind, ran end-to-end along Ontario's majestic Bruce Trail. The total distance covered was nine hundred kilometers (560 miles) in twenty days. The Bruce Trail is known for not only its tranquil beauty but also its unforgiving and technical terrain. Rhonda amassed a team of over fifty volunteers to assist her as support crew and guide-runners for her epic journey. I had the honor of being a guide-runner for a forty-five-kilometer (twenty-eight-mile) leg of Rhonda-Marie's journey. When it comes to a definition of resilience, I think Rhonda-Marie is the embodiment of the power of eternal optimism and the enduring human spirit.

I run to remember I'm alive, that it's okay I take up space, and that I am worthy of taking up that space. I run because "they" think I won't—because it's not expected, because it's not accepted. I run to remember I'm hungry. I run to remind myself that life can be good, and special, and kind. I run to be present in my life, and I run to spend forever learning about myself—the good, the bad, and the ugly about myself. I run to find the edges of myself. I run to change the edges of myself. I run in the hope of being able to accept love, and to someday love myself.

People often joke that running is cheaper than therapy. I ran through coping with my husband's affair. I ran through the inevitable fallout of my marriage. I used running to navigate the scary dark corners in my head. When the lonely forest terrifies me, I slip inside the bits of me I'd like to keep hidden and know that there is little reason to fear a landscape. I run to recover from an eating disorder. Don't believe me? Try running fifty kilometers while eating nothing. Survival makes the balance shift. Reality comes into focus. I use running to create awareness for disabled athletes, to help shift a norm ever so slightly.

Blind running means I am almost never alone—or shouldn't be. I most certainly don't race alone. A running tribe is how I get to experience this wonderful "run thing." It's easier not to slip over an edge of darkness when surrounded by a group. Also the tribe creates change, and for me, that means moving disability into a more mainstream thinking.

I'm affectionately known as Batgirl in the running community because I do most of my running in the dark when my limited vision is at its best. I like to call my kids my Batcubs, and I want them to grow up in a world where Mom tries—a world where the disabled aren't shunned away from an entire genre just because it's not a good fit. And fear. Fear inspires me to keep going. I won't cross the busy road at noon to go get groceries, but I'll run in the forest for twenty hours. I can't be afraid to live.

When it comes to leaving my running footprint on the community, I would like it to be *awareness*. I'd love to create this place for people to dialogue about disability and sport. Not a special place— just a normal everyday space, a tipping point.

Running has helped me accept myself in my own skin. *Disabled* means "different." We don't shy away from pointing that out, from fearing it, shunning it, shutting it out. Learning to accept the idea that I haven't failed at being human simply due to my lack of standard vision is an everyday struggle, but running certainly helps with that.

My proudest achievement as a runner was convincing 50 people to rearrange their lives to come out to support me and to guide-run huge distances along the Bruce Trail. If 50 people showed up, 100 others thought about it. If 150 people were involved, 500 knew about it. And if 500 people talked for one minute about disability and sport, then I consider that a start.

HAVING FAITH IN A POWER
GREATER THAN YOURSELF
SARA'S STORY

Author's note: Sara Hall is a professional American middle-distance runner. In 2011, she won the 3,000-meter steeplechase in 10:03 at the Pan American Games in Guadalajara, Mexico, while representing the United States. Sara is married to the elite US marathoner Ryan Hall, so I was overjoyed that they both found time in their busy schedules to share a little bit about how they nurture their relationship as a couple while balancing the emotional and physical demands of elite training and media commitments, not to mention the highs and lows of competing on the world stage.

It has actually been a huge blessing to be full-time athletes in that we are able to spend almost all day together every day, and that has really allowed us to form a solid foundation in our first years of marriage. We have gotten to travel the world together and experience a lot of incredible things early on in our marriage.

We have also had to really step up our support of each other since leaving a team and going out on our own five years ago. Our running is now a journey we are on together—one in which we feel very much we are approaching as a team. Of course, we feel the burden when the other person is struggling with injuries or fatigue, but I think knowing exactly what the other person is going through allows us to sympathize and also support in the best way possible.

Building resilience is the number one character trait I will take away from this career and bring into whatever I tackle next in life. I have been through a lot of huge disappointments and failures, and through the process, I have learned that my identity can't be in my performances. Really experiencing God's love for me, and learning how He created me, has allowed my identity to be unshakable by bad races. I now go into competitions fearless and able to take big risks because my whole identity isn't at stake. And when a big race doesn't go as planned, I'm still bummed, but I can pick myself up and hope and dream again with God because with Him, there is always hope.

FAITH TO RISE AGAIN
RYAN'S STORY

Author's note: Ryan Hall is a professional American long-distance runner. In 2008, he won the marathon at the US Olympic Trials, and went on to place tenth in the Olympic marathon in Beijing. He currently holds the US record in the half marathon. At the 2011 Boston Marathon, Ryan Hall ran a time of 2:04:58, which is the fastest marathon ever run by an American. Unfortunately, despite Hall's incredible achievement, Boston's point-to-point net-elevation-loss course makes it ineligible for record purposes. In 2009, Ryan and his wife, Sara, formed the Hall Steps Foundation—a community activist organization that engages the running community to use the same energy and resources that fuel their athletic achievements for social justice efforts.

My favorite Bible verse says, "Though a righteous man falls seven times, he rises again." Running requires resilience because the journey of any runner is full of incredible disappointments, heartbreak, and setbacks, but it's in the struggle that we grow. I'm learning to look at my shortcomings as amazing opportunities for me to grow and get stronger.

My advice to someone hoping to build a strong and supportive running community is to surround yourself with people you want to be like. We moved to Redding, California, so that we would be surrounded by people we want to be like. I chose to go to Stanford University largely because of the quality of people there. So surround yourself with greatness and also with people who are going after the same things you are going after.

ADDING ANOTHER DAY OR TWO TO MY LIFE
GREG'S STORY

I run to clear the clutter of my mind from the day-to-day stress of life. Running puts all my stress into perspective. I run because I can do it anywhere in the world as long as I have a good pair of shoes. I run because I don't need to join a team or buy a lot of gear. I love the simplicity of putting one foot in front of another for an extended period of time. After a good run, I feel like I've added another day or two to my life. I run to experience those incredible moments in a day as the sun rises and I get to witness nature in all its glory . . . when it's just me, the breeze on my back, the color of the sky, and that beautiful hawk that seems to follow me.

Fitness is a lifestyle for me. I run because I'm inspired by other people to stay fit, and by doing so, I know I inspire others to do the same. Running makes me feel alive! As a musician, when I run, I feel the rhythm of my breath and the pace of my stride as my feet strike the pavement. This rhythm grounds me and becomes almost meditative to me.

As a victim of childhood sexual abuse, my life has been forever changed. I have feelings such as: an extreme sense of guilt and shame, low self-esteem, self -doubt, helplessness, difficulties with re-lationships, depression, mood swings, anxiety, and fear, just to name a few. Running is my outlet. It is the one thing I felt I have control over—something I can do on my own to help me cope with my anx-iety and emotions. Setting a running goal, planning for races, training, then meeting those goals provides me with a means to nurture myself in a way that alcohol, drugs, or other addictive behaviors could never do. Running marathons lifts me emotionally. It gives me a huge pay-off by elevating my self-esteem, by showing me I can accomplish something pretty profound, something that many people can't or choose not to do, and that act alone lifts me and heals me.

I recognize that my abuse will affect me the rest of my life. There will be times when I'm strong against its negative impact, and times when I am weak and triggered. As a fitness lifestyle, running will always be in my life to help me when things are dark, when I am in my shadow, and when I need a gift from me to me.

IT'S ONLY THE TIP OF THE ICEBERG
JOSE'S STORY

We have all heard the benefits of running, walking, cycling, and swimming. And those who participate in these sports have their reasons—to look better or feel better would probably be among the top two. My reason? Because I enjoy getting out, not to mention the feeling and energy I get from being active. I will never be an elite athlete. I don't want to; that's not on my to-do list, and there are far too many other things on that list. But during the past two years, that list has tripled. Why? How? Well, two years ago, my wife and I adopted three siblings from Colombia. So, you might ask, "How does that tie in with running?" "Does it have something to do with being healthy?" Or for that matter, "How do I find the time?"

Since the adoption, life has changed drastically for my wife and me. The life of an adoptive family is like an iceberg. There is so much of what is seen at the surface, but much more that lies underwater. Our children were four, eight, and eleven at the time of the adoption. At that age, they are already well aware of their life; the two older children still have clear memories of being put up for adoption, and no doubt that leaves deep emotional scars. That's what lies under the iceberg of our family life. Everyone sees the happy family—lots of love and smiles. But there are days of complete chaos.

Not many are aware of that, just a handful of our closest friends with whom we sometimes chat to vent off some steam, frustration, and sadness . . . Sometimes it's tough to keep things together.

I am fortunate to work about ten kilometers from home. That is the perfect running or cycling distance. Family life is very busy, not only daily activities, but extracurricular activities too. My kids play several sports and are involved in various groups. Plus coming from South America, they have a new language to learn (not to mention English). All their homework is in Swedish, so each of them requires help with translating. My time for exercising is not only zero, but into the negatives once I get back home. So what I do instead is use my commute to and from work to exercise. I wake up earlier to get on the bike, or lace up my running shoes.

The feeling after a good run or bike ride is great. It clears my mind. It allows me to step back for a second to catch my breath and exhale some stress. I get the chance to inhale a boost of energy that I really need at times. Parents are busy and stressed as it is, but adoptive parents, well that adds another layer. Running has helped me stay fit, and it has helped me psychologically. I can endure much more mentally and emotionally without feeling as drained as before. As they say, "a strong body, a strong mind, and a strong soul." That's perhaps how I can best describe it. Running takes me to that place where I can clean my mind, rinse away my problems, breathe in life, and just feel good. But what happens when I stop running? I don't know—I haven't stopped. There have been a few weeks off here and there, but the long-term effects are present during those days too.

Running has given me the strength to be a good father, husband, friend, and co-worker. To others, it might be painting, playing an instrument, yoga, knitting . . . anything. We all have that place to go where we feel better. My place is wherever my feet or bike take me.

FEELING ALIVE IN GREAT PAIN
DEAN'S STORY

Author's note: Dean Karnazes, who has been referred to as "the fittest man on the planet," was named by Time *magazine as one of the 100 Most Influential People in the World. As an internationally recognized endurance athlete and best-selling author, Dean continues to demonstrate the incredible resilience of the human body and the ability of the mind to push the body to inconceivable limits. Among Dean's astounding running feats are, running 350 continuous miles (563 kilometers), forgoing sleep for three nights, running across Death Valley in 120°F (49°C) temperatures, and running a marathon to the South Pole in –40°F (–40°C). One of his more publicized endeavors was running fifty marathons in all fifty US states, on fifty consecutive days. Oh yeah, and he topped that off by finishing with the New York City Marathon in a time of three hours!*

Running has taught me that I can get through tough situations and persevere. It has also taught me that there is magic in misery. Never do I feel more alive and in touch with the universe than when I am struggling and in great pain. I have learned to embrace the difficult moments, for those are the ones that define us.

Anything that gets people outside and moving is a good thing. Elite athletes tend to be highly self-motivated, but that might not be the case for all people. They may need that nudge, and running groups and clinics provide that support. However, I think it largely depends on your personality traits. Introverts often prefer to train on their own, and that's just fine. My guidance to other runners is always: Listen to everyone; follow no one. Do what works best for you.

IN LOSS, SOMETHING IS FOUND
LAURIE ANN'S STORY

My relationship with running is multifaceted. There are times when running embodies my running away from something, yet in that, I'm running toward something else. Sometimes running is about picking up the pieces—take grief as an example. For me, it isn't just about the kilometers I put in; it's about something bigger than that. My relationship with running is something that makes me feel whole, confident, and alive. Running brings health to my body, clarity to my mind, and peace to my spirit.

When I first started running, it was about trying to do something I thought I couldn't do. You see, there was a time in my life where I was close to four hundred pounds, so losing almost half my body weight and being able to run was monumental in and of itself. Being a runner was something I never imagined I could do, in fact I used to refuse to run in middle school gym class. I remember my teacher, Ms. Bridge, encouraging me to just try, but I thought it was too hard, so I gave up on myself. When I decided to run my first 5K, I thought of her and resolved that I would complete one race in support of the Juvenile Diabetes Research Foundation and then I'd never have to run again.

After the first race, I was hooked and I signed up for more; however, I became very hard on myself because I felt that I had to run faster and harder to be accepted as a real runner. It was too much pressure, but later I came to understand that it doesn't matter what others think; it is what I think that counts. Part of my evolution as a runner has been to let go of that competitive side and get back to the fun of running. As I grew, I discovered that I had nothing to prove to others and being the best version of myself was what is important. The competition, as they say, isn't with other runners; it is with myself.

Running has affected every area of my life. It makes me a better mom and wife because I am taking care of myself. Being a runner literally saved my life. It has allowed me to develop a sense of belonging to a community that does so much in the line of being charitable. It has given me the courage to be open to new activities and challenges. Running has influenced our family's nutritional choices and taught us the importance of rest. When I don't nourish my body well, it shows in my runs. When I eat well and sleep well, it reduces stress, anxiety, and depression; and that in turn helps me deal with the side effects of diabetes and heart disease. It has taught me that failure isn't the end of the world and that great personal growth comes from falling down and getting back up. Running is about so much more than running.

I could write an entire chapter on the mental benefits of running, but I'll try to sum it up as briefly as I can. Of course, the more obvious side effects, for me at least, are increased self-esteem from the sense of accomplishment and combating the blues. It's hard to feel sad when I'm out on my favorite trail listening to my iPod or the awakening sounds of the forest. There really isn't anything pharmacological that can replicate that with such positive side effects. I've experienced a lot of loss. Both my parents and three of my siblings have passed away. I've been physically and sexually assaulted. Our home burned to the ground. Add miscarriages, a diagnosis of diabetes, and a heart problem to that, and sometimes things have been downright depressing.

The physiological aspect of exercise is that it can be, at least for me, like a natural antidepressant. For some reason when I run, it seems to make everything appear better. For example, after my mom passed away, I trained for my first half marathon as a way to escape the overwhelming emotion from the horrible emptiness I was feeling. She was my best friend, and we chatted every morning without fail.

That was suddenly gone, and it left a huge void, not just in my heart, but in my time. I filled that void with running so that I could attempt to find a place where I could start to heal. At first, I was running from the emotional pain, and then one day that shifted. I was running along a trail through the woods next to the Grand River when I saw a cardinal, her favorite bird. It felt as though the cardinal was following me, and I was instantly reminded of our walks in the woods together when I was little. I headed out on the next runs reminiscing about those times rather than running away from the grief.

Another way that running helps with mental illness is from a support perspective. Runners are some of the most supportive and inclusive people I've met. When I see runners who have overcome great hardships, it makes me feel like I can too. There is a camaraderie there, not just in lacing up but with life itself. Every runner has a story, and so many of us have used running as a way of healing. I find that runners lift each other up, and that sense of community is something I treasure.

GOING TO THE IMPOSSIBLE
RAY'S STORY

Author's note: Ray Zahab is a legendary Canadian long-distance runner and motivational speaker. On November 1, 2006, Ray and two friends, Charlie Engle and Kevin Lin, set out on an expedition to cross the Sahara Desert by foot. One hundred eleven days and seventy-five hundred kilometers (forty-seven hundred miles) after leaving the coast of Senegal, Africa, they completed their epic journey by stepping into the Red Sea. In 2008, Ray founded impossible2Possible (i2P), an organization that aims to inspire and educate youth through adventure learning, inclusion, and participation in expeditions.

I've often said that running has been my greatest teacher. When I say this, I mean it literally! Running has taught me that we *all* have the capacity to exceed limits we think we might have. When I began running, I wasn't sure I could do it, but it became my life, and has taught me so much about myself, and others. Whether it's learning through adventure, or learning about myself, running has been a true gift in my life.

A DEEPER UNDERSTANDING OF WHO YOU ARE
MARA'S STORY

When I started running, I was out to prove something. Later I realized how hard it is, especially when it comes to endurance running, and that I'd have to be doing it for reasons besides external validation. After I went through a really bad depressive episode in the summer of 2014, my relationship with running really changed for the better. Instead of berating myself to finish miles, I've learned—and am continually learning—to use my running as a way to be kind to myself. So I'm running toward healing, I suppose, but I know that I'll never actually get there because life is always evolving and never permanent.

There will always be something I have to heal from, especially as someone who struggles with mental health issues, and I hope running can be a part of that process for as much of my life as possible. The biggest lesson running has taught me is acceptance of all things, good and bad. It was really hard for me, at first, to accept that there would be really bad runs, slow runs, and difficult runs. I would berate myself for not being stronger, faster, and better, but that kind of thinking doesn't get you anywhere, or at least it doesn't get me anywhere. Whenever I can, I now try to motivate myself through positivity and self-compassion: positivity for every accomplishment, big and small, and self-compassion for those really tough runs, for the unfinished runs, and for all of the pain that comes with running (and there is a lot of it). And sometimes, though not always, this mind-set seeps into other parts of my thinking and life.

I am absolutely and 100 percent in favor of promoting exercise as a way to improve mental illness, self-worth, and overall well-being. That being said, I think it needs to be promoted with a healing mind-set. I see too many people struggle to get into an exercise routine only to be shamed into quitting because they think they're not good enough. If we're not careful, exercise can become another way to be hard on ourselves, and that is especially dangerous for anyone who struggles with mental illness. I remember times when I couldn't finish a run, and the inadequacy I felt would spiral into a really bad bout of self-criticism and self-destructive behavior, and that would ironi-cally really hinder me from wanting to run again, for which I'd further berate myself. It's a really vicious cycle. Nevertheless, done with com-passion and positivity, I think exercise, and running in particular, can be part of the most vital treatment for anyone who struggles with mental health issues.

Running teaches us how to hold both good and bad at the same time (*man, my legs really hurt, but gosh it is a beautiful day!*). It is the ultimate biological exploration of your mind . . . convincing it that it can go farther even though every part of you wants to stop. Endurance running in particular creates a sort of resilience and awareness of your thought processes and a deeper understanding of who you are and how you react to the world around you—something that can be very hard to come by when you struggle with mental health.

Running has made me resilient in more ways than I can count. Not only am I physically healthier, but also it's made it easier for me to accept anger, sadness, fear, and loss. Bad days are just a little better if I've gone for a run. For me, it really is all about acceptance and developing a non-judgmental awareness of life, what happens in it, and my own feelings. I am a firm believer in approaching running with a mind of meditation, and this has translated into me being far more stable and content than I was prior to becoming a runner. This is by no means saying my life is in any way on a consistently linear trajectory toward total happiness. It's just that because running itself comes laden with so many necessary pains and angst, it is a lot easier to accept the necessary pains and angst of life as well.

THE ART OF SELF-DISCOVERY
ANN'S STORY

I grew up in a horribly abusive environment. But I do not like to think of myself as running away from that; instead, I think of myself as running toward the better me.

Running has made me a better, more capable person. Through running, I've learned self-examination. Running gives me the time to think about my life, what happened in the past, and how I can make my future better. When I was a young runner (twenty-five years ago), I spent a lot of my running hours thinking over ways to be a better mom. I still do that, but now that my kids are older, I use it to think about advancing my career and being a better writer.

For years, I ran to reduce stress. Whenever I had a tough day, I would go for a run. If I found myself angry with someone, I would run before talking to the person as a way to mitigate the anger. But two years ago, I discovered that my daughter was self-harming and had become suicidal. She had to be hospitalized. That first hospitalization was just the beginning, though. For the next two years, our lives revolved around this situation. It was incredibly stressful. Unfortunately, in the beginning I became hypervigilant—I couldn't sleep. I couldn't eat. Every time I closed my eyes I pictured finding my daughter dead. At its height, I began to realize that running was not helping at all. I would go for a run, but become so stressed that I couldn't breathe. Luckily something clicked for me on one of these runs. Suddenly I realized that if running was not helping, I really needed to seek professional help for myself. That being said, I allowed the doctors to put me on antidepressants for a few months, and in truth, I wish I hadn't. What I needed was rest. I needed a break from being "in charge" of my daughter's mental state. I needed a therapist. I didn't need drugs.

One of the stories I tell a lot is about sitting at the dinner table with my mom and a group of friends and their moms. All of these girls were in the beauty pageant scene. The moms started telling my mom how I should enter one of these pageants. My mom scoffed. She told them not only did I not have a single talent but I was the biggest klutz she had ever seen. The funny thing is that we both believed that. Over the years, all of the bruises and lash marks she had left on my body—all of the stitches and broken bones—had all been chalked up to "accidents." "Ann fell again. Ann ran into the door again." Somehow I had grown to believe I was truly a klutz.

Running my first marathon was eye opening for me. I did have a talent. I could run, and I could do it without falling on my face. It was actually during that first marathon that it occurred to me that I was not really klutzy and had never been klutzy. I had just bought into the stories we had always told the authorities.

I don't know many runners who haven't been sidelined by injury, illness, or family circumstances. I used to complain about it to anybody who would listen, but during the time that my daughter was struggling the most, I realized that not only was running not helping but in some ways it was hurting. I was putting so much pressure on myself to keep running that I was no longer enjoying it. During that period, I took some time off. Coming back from that has been so much harder than I expected, but I am getting there, and the best part is that I am enjoying running again. I am not stressed out by it. I can do it without the pressure I felt before. My advice is to breathe. Take a minute to decide what else you can do while you are sidelined. The thing I hear most often from other runners is how much cleaner their houses are when they have to take time off from running.

AT TIMES, EVEN THE THERAPIST NEEDS TO BECOME THE CLIENT
ELISE'S STORY

When I've had major injuries, I've gone through big mental stress. Almost more than the physical pain is the pain of not being able to run. Running is healing, and for many of us, it's a way to maintain our physical fitness and body.

It was not until my latest major injury that I learned so much about myself. Why was I training so hard and driving myself into the ground? I looked inside to see the reason behind it. I had lost about thirteen pounds after my foot surgery, but I had a recurrence of an eating disorder. At the time, I did not want to admit it, but now that I am healing, I can see through it.

I won my age group at many local triathlons, and placed second at a half Ironman in New York, and I had even set my sights on qualifying for the Half Ironman World Championships. I trained at any cost regardless of how I felt. Taking a day off was torture. Then the big injuries began to happen, and I realized that I was not a happy person trying to do this. It was affecting my relationships and other parts of my life.

It was not until I was in the throes of this injury that I could finally see this. Now I am far more aware and in tune. I use yoga to calm my mind and settle my body. I take days off without guilt. I fuel well, and eat intuitively instead of sticking to a solid inflexible plan. I enjoy food more and have learned to get rid of negative thoughts. I am okay with not being that fast anymore. Being injury-free for the last year feels good. My bone density has improved, and other health markers have returned to normal. I can honestly say I have learned so much about myself through this latest injury.

I'm a physiotherapist, and it was very frustrating to know so much and to not be able to be objective about my own injury. I had to rely on others to guide me, and I had to start treating myself like a client, and not the therapist.

I now feel that if I were to face any future setback, I would be able to handle it better. I would focus on what I can do, and listen to my body. I do whatever I can now to limit stress and the onset of cortisol (stress hormone), as I feel like this is a dangerous thing. I also hope that with my new outlook and an awareness of when my body needs rest, that I will be able to avert any major future setbacks. Part of this has meant hiring a coach to keep me in check, and to keep me from overtraining. I've also come to understand that my body does have its limits, and those need to be respected. At my age, I want to be able to run long into my later adult years, and this requires respecting my mechanical limits.

FROM DURBAN TO PIETERMARITZBURG
AND BACK AGAIN
BRUCE'S STORY

Author's note: Bruce Fordyce is a South African marathon and ultramarathon athlete, but more accurately can be described as a running legend. He is best known for having won the South African Comrades Marathon (an eighty-nine-kilometer race up and down unrelenting mountainous terrain in South Africa) a record nine times, eight of which were consecutive. Bruce has also won the London to Brighton Marathon three years in a row. He currently holds the world fifty-mile record and is the former world record holder for one hundred kilometers. I've had the pleasure of meeting Bruce on a few occasions, and hearing his talk in Durban, South Africa, was definitely one of the highlights of my Comrades Marathon experience. In this interview, Bruce has chosen to describe himself as a "marathon runner, businessman, and dad." I consider Bruce to be a treasure to the running community: Unlike most elite athletes who often disappear from the running scene after their competitive career begins to wane, Bruce has remained active and involved in sharing his passion for running with the entire world. If you ever have the opportunity to hear him speak, believe me, you won't be disappointed.

I am definitely running toward something: toward a healthier longer life, a good finishing time in next year's Two Oceans Race, and a happy, productive day after my run.

I used to train very hard twice a day (160 to 240 kilometers per week), but now I run once a day, probably 60 to 70 kilometers a week. Following a bad knee injury, one that three experienced surgeons were convinced would end my running days, my running has taught me I can achieve anything I want. And after a year of rehab, I am running again. I run with a limp, but my goal is next year's Two Oceans fifty-six-kilometer race, and it will be my thirty-first Two Oceans.

Certainly the most important part of my running is the time I spend on my own with my thoughts. When angry or frustrated, I find running is very therapeutic. I run mostly on my own, but sometimes with others as well. In my role as an ambassador for the Comrades Marathon, I would definitely classify myself as a leader/gatherer.

Running has made me very resilient because it has taught me I can get through anything if I set my mind to the task. As I mentioned previously, I have been sidelined for a year with a bad knee injury, and I am not fully recovered yet, but I am gradually getting back from "no hope" to my first half marathon in over a year coming up in just ten days' time. Interestingly, it is the Kruger Park Half Marathon, where we run in the reserve and rangers have to guard us at every corner so we don't get taken out by an elephant or lion. I will get through it the same way we run marathons—one step at a time, one small victory at a time, and I'll be prepared for the odd setback.

SOMETHING TO HELP ME DO WHAT NON-ADDICTS CAN DO INNATELY
CHRISTA'S STORY

I run to stay sober and to be less burdened by the effects of depression. Reward and punishment are two sides of the same coin for me. I am wired to categorize all things as good or bad; positive or negative; rewardable or punishable. Alcohol became the solution that supplied the laughs at the celebration and tears at the pity party, and those weren't necessarily mutually exclusive events. Alcohol was the remedy for emotions, high and low. It was a coping tool or more accurately a tool I used not to cope.

Today, after four and a half years of fragile sobriety, running has replaced alcohol. Running is what soothes my emotions and keeps me balanced, but the underlying wiring is still there. I run to celebrate, and I run to punish. I can run with joy in my heart and in my step, or I can run with anger and tears pouring out of me. Whether I run happy or I run sad, I usually have some kind of control or perspective on my thoughts and emotions when I am done.

Nothing externally changes because I run; the shift happens internally. At the end of a run, nothing is ever as good or bad as it seemed at the beginning. By the end of a run, there is no good or bad, no positive or negative, and no more reward or punishment; things, events, and emotions are just what they are without judgment or labels. Running changes my perspective, not my reality, just as alcohol once did. I am still a slave to needing something to help me do what non-addicts can do innately, but at least the choice I make to run is a solution doesn't hurt anyone else.

I accept that I may never run as fast as I like, and that I may never win my age group at any race. I let that go with my latest injury. It is just so hard to take two steps forward toward improvement and then be knocked back a step by an injury. I am working on being happy with my efforts no matter what they are on any particular day, and that leads me to the understanding that it is more important to me to just be able to run at all, never mind how fast.

I've had to be incredibly resilient when it comes to my alcoholism. I don't really think that you ever overcome the sauce, because it's always waiting for you. More accurately, running has helped me overcome how I see alcohol and its relationship to my life. Running helps me clearly see that the good old drunken days were not as good as I thought they were.

I suppose my first marathon was my greatest running achievement. It was tough, but I did it anyway. Doing the tough stuff is what builds confidence and is satisfying well beyond the pain and sacrifice it took to secure the achievement. The moment I crossed the finish line, I knew I had done something big. I saw myself differently.

I WASN'T GOOD ENOUGH YET!
NATE'S STORY

Author's note: Nate Jenkins describes himself as a "teacher and former professional runner." Nate has a marathon PB of 2:14 and finished seventh at the 2008 US Olympic Trials Marathon. I've been following Nate's journey for many years now, and what I've always admired about him is his ability to speak openly and write about the physical and mental toll that comes with being a high-profile elite athlete.

On my runs I tend to obsess on the future—upcoming races, sometimes years in the future, upcoming work plans, financial plans, life goals. But all the time if you were recording my thoughts, the overarching theme would be that I seem to be running away from where I'm from and how I grew up. I don't want to make it sound like I had it really rough; I didn't. I just wasn't happy and didn't feel secure, or exceptional, or important, and all those things mattered to me.

I started running 1 to 2 miles four to five days a week in elementary school, and over the years I built up to a point where I regularly ran over 160 miles a week, and then to the point at which I considered anytime where I did less than a "10 and 10 double" to be a rare occurrence. Generally speaking, my running has always been with a goal in mind, so what I do is directly designed to shape my body to the physical task that is my next goal race or season—and did it ever shape me! I am a person who has a great personal fire and competitiveness that at times has felt like it would tear me apart from the inside out. Running was, and is, its outlet. It helps me focus, de-stress, and control that fire. Without running, I would be lost. Almost from the moment I first did it, I felt very strongly that it was a core aspect of my personal self-definition.

I have no medical or psychological training or expertise, so I can only speak from personal experience—without running, I certainly would not be functioning in society on a very normal level. By running, I control and push through my tendency toward depression. It has taught me patience, understanding, and humility, all of which shape every interaction I have in the world.

When I started running, I did it because I wanted to win, needed to win. The thing is, I didn't win. I had been a regular runner for literally years before I won a race. With running, there was always another race. I could always train a little more and come back better the next time, the next season, the next year. I could get hurt and then heal and become stronger than before. Again and again, the lesson of each failure wasn't that I wasn't good enough, or that I wasn't a champion, it was that I wasn't good enough *yet*. I wasn't a champion *yet*. So I would always turn to the next goal, the bigger goal, and eventually I learned to have faith in this process of never taking a failure too close to heart, of always viewing each failure as a chance to learn and a stepping-stone toward future successes that would be even greater.

In college, I had a number of injuries that caused me to miss long stretches of running. I never got through it well. The most positive solution I came up with was trying to cross-train into the ground. Now I tend to go to yoga a lot. It shortens the injury, and it gives me some of the same mental and emotional benefits. My other solutions were always destructive—drinking, eating, dieting, and other poor choices. So for me, although I feel very satisfied, happy, and at peace in my life without running, that balance slowly disappears, and I drift toward becoming a person I do not like very much.

Sidelined, Sabotaged, and Sidetracked

The very essence of romance is uncertainty.
—Oscar Wilde

As we've seen throughout this book, running is so much more than merely a physical pursuit—it's a way of life or, more accurately, a way of being within your life. We run to make us happy. We run to extinguish our anger and resentment. We run to escape, and we run to find ourselves. For many of us, running is our best friend, our faithful companion, that ever-present soundtrack to our life. But what happens when your best friend suddenly drops out of the picture, no longer returns your calls, leaves you in the lurch? As bitter a pill as this may be to swallow, there is no denying that there comes a time in your life as a runner when an illness, injury, or outside circumstance will force you to stop running—either temporarily or permanently.

A sidelined runner embarks upon a journey far beyond mending broken bones, tending to damaged tendons, or recuperating from illness. It's a journey that takes place as much in the mind as it does it in the body. With all the time we athletes devote to our physical training and sport-specific skill set, it's hardly surprising that we are sorely wanting when it comes to managing the emotional toll of pro-longed and demoralizing downtime.

But not all is lost—nurturing and incorporating a few strategies necessary to honing your mental acuity will go a long way to speeding recovery and returning you to your chosen sport. That being said, if not addressed, the mental and emotional repercussions of an injury or illness may have more long-lasting effects than the physical trauma itself.

Runners invest much of themselves in the pursuit of their sport, and in turn define themselves by that interaction with the sport. When injury, illness, or life circumstances disrupt that delicate bal-ance, the sidelined runner endures a profound sense of emptiness including: loss of identify, loss of role or position, loss of belonging, loss of structure and routine, loss of future goals, and—most of all—loss of mastery or a feeling of control.

In order to achieve some modicum of success or fulfillment, the social and psychological traits that we runners bring to our sport are, ironically, the same characteristics that hinder our recovery from in-jury or illness. We can see each as a two-sided coin, one constructive, the other destructive. *Motivation* creates an intense focus and drive to excel, but unrestrained can lead to overtraining and obsessive run-ning. *Arousal* activates that force inside us, that inner passion that permits us to walk the treacherous tightrope toward the outer limits of our endurance. Yet if we are not careful, the stimulus effect of this heightened arousal quickly manifests as stress and anxiety. When we reach this negative state, we default to self-questioning, perfectionism, and the inevitable slide into physical and mental dysfunction.

So, God forbid, suppose the unimaginable has occurred and you are compelled to stop running—you are sidelined and your reality has been significantly altered. You have arrived at ground zero, so it's now time to embrace your new reality and if possible, begin to craft the art of a comeback.

As is the case anytime the rug has been pulled out from under you, it's natural that you will gravitate toward stinkin' thinkin'; cue the melancholy refrain of the pity parade that will become your life. You might as well get used to saying good-bye to the regular dose of adrenaline-soaked endorphins that running brought into your life, and prepare yourself for the potential weight gain and muscle atrophy that often accompany significant downtime.

For all you addicts out there, be warned—you may have just lost your one remaining sanity outlet, the misdirection that has allowed you to get through the day without doing harm to yourself or others. You're now faced with one burning question—*Who am I without running?* To make matters even worse, many of us athletes have chosen to permanently mark our skin with a running tattoo. What may have at one time been a badge of pride now stares us in the face as a burning reminder of the thing that has been so cruelly taken away from us. Let's just pray it's a temporary absence.

Whenever anyone, or in this case anything, is suddenly taken from us, it's reasonable that we look for a meaningful response to this loss, or at least a road map with which to crawl our way out of this misfortune. A few years back, *Runner's World* ran an article that compared getting through a running injury to moving through the stages of grief: denial, anger, bargaining, depression, and acceptance. Funny as that sounds, I don't think they were far off the mark in describing the manic purgatory that we sidelined runners find ourselves in.

Oh, the slippery slope of denial is a place with which most of us runners are intimately acquainted. It starts off with you trying to silence the signals, cues, and alarms radiating from your body as it tells you it's time to shut your running down for a while. The typical refrain is "It's not that bad. I can run through this." Depending on the severity of your injury, this can go on for weeks until the burning pain leaves that unmistakable metallic taste in your mouth that you can no longer ignore. I hate to be the bearer of bad news, but you're not about to find much reprieve as you reluctantly move into the next phase—anger. If you're in a relationship with a runner in this stage, now is a good time to take cover and lie low for a bit. This is the point at which the inconsolable runner finally realizes that he or she doesn't just like to run, but actually needs to run. Facing all these extra hours of unstructured time in the week leaves us desperate to fill the void with tasks like cleaning the house, paying bills, and reaching out to people whom we haven't spoken to in months. And there is coffee . . . lots and lots of coffee.

When you're finished being angry, or—more accurately—when everyone around you is sick and tired of you walking around like a raging toddler, you move into the next stage: bargaining. I like to refer to this phase as the *I'll sell my soul to the Devil if* stage. Seriously . . . you are willing to do anything to get back into running, and that even includes those stretches and strength-building exercises you "politely" told your physiotherapist you would do two weeks ago when you were still basking in the naive glow of denial.

Then, just as things are starting to look up, you discover that you are not the center of the universe—that in fact you are not able to simply bargain your way back into running. Welcome to the fourth stage of running grief—depression. Ah . . . I know it well. This is the time I go into deep, deep hiding. I can't look at Facebook or Twitter because reading all my friends' running posts, and seeing all their running selfies, is like a slow, toxic death by a thousand cuts. But there does come a day when you decide that the self-imposed exile has run its course, and that maybe, just maybe, you're ready to join the human species again—welcome to the final stage, acceptance. You've been sidelined and sabotaged, but now you've arrived at a place of peace and serenity. Well . . . no . . . you'll more than likely never arrive there, but at least you've accepted that running is not in the cards at the moment.

I thought I would share with you my tried-and-true secret strategy guaranteed to get you back to running 50 percent sooner. Are you kidding me . . . no such thing exists, but the fact that your brain told you there *might* be one clearly indicates you are still in the denial stage. There are, however, a few things you might consider letting go of in order to make your downtime a little more bearable.

First off, stop beating yourself up about what you could have or should have done differently—it's a complete waste of energy that could be better spent in laying the groundwork for your return to activity. That brings me to the next point: time lines. Recovery takes as long as it takes, so dropping the artificial return date will help relieve a lot of that stress you're under. Finally, you are not letting down your family, teammates, and friends simply because you are unable to run. Running is all about creating greatness inside us. Try to remind yourself that greatness does not come without toil, sweat, and the occasional heartbreak.

The road back to running, or for that matter any sport after a prolonged layoff, is not without its hills and valleys, and its crags and potholes. Like it or not, rehab is not a race—doubling up on icing or the number of stretches will probably not get you back on the road any quicker. My years as a competitive athlete have taught me four essential truths of every injury. First, the sooner you become an "injury whisperer," the better. Instead of being frustrated at being sidelined yet again, listen to what your injury is trying to tell you. Is there something you need to tweak, change, or discard in terms of your diet, training, or lifestyle? Second, for whatever reason, if you're not able to run, don't go into hiding. Stay connected to the sport and reach out to other runners for support, and—most important—remember that this is the time to give back to our sport by volunteering at a race or by acknowledging the successes that others have achieved. Next, hone your mental imagery skills, not only by visualizing your return to the start line but also by satisfying your running fix via watching inspirational movies and videos that get your competitive juices flowing again. Finally, harness all that frustration you are feeling and direct it toward laying out some sport-specific goals and benchmarks. This is the ideal time to reevaluate your running practice so that when you do return, you're ready to hit the ground running.

When I sat down to write this book, I knew that there would need to be a chapter addressing illness and running injuries, but to be brutally honest I wasn't looking forward to the depressing subject matter and self-absorbed pity parade. I sent out a request on social media for stories from the running community on dealing with prolonged absence from running due to illness, injury, and life circumstances. I then sat back and waited for my inbox to be flooded with tales of sadness, misery, and grief. Boy, was I wrong! Instead, I was inundated by the most remarkable accounts of inspiration, motivation, and acceptance. In the remainder of this chapter, I would like to share some of these stories with you in the hope that within each of these voices, you'll find a kernel of truth you've been searching for. Hopefully, you'll find yourself in the words of these amazing runners.

SETTING GOALS AND LIVING A FULL LIFE
AFTER A DIAGNOSIS OF RRMS
JENNIFER'S STORY

I am a runner who has been diagnosed with RRMS (relapsing-remitting multiple sclerosis—the most common form of multiple sclerosis). MS is an autoimmune disease that causes inflammation of the insulating membranes (myelin) that surround nerves within the central nervous system. When I was diagnosed back in late 2011, I was training for my first half marathon at the Toronto Waterfront race.

I thought my athletic career was over when I heard my diagnosis. But since then, I have run countless half marathons, a full marathon, and now I am training for a 50K race this fall. The road hasn't always been easy. Running can sometimes be painful, or my fatigue hits so hard that walking to my bathroom is a chore, never mind a 10K tempo run that my schedule calls for. I truly do feel that my stubbornness to keep at it has slowed down the progression of my disease, and I live a very active and healthy life because of it. Also, my last MRI showed no new lesions for the first time in four years!

I always think that my disease could be worse. I could have more frequent attacks or even lose the ability to walk. That is always on the radar, but for now, I just keep on running and setting more goals for myself fitness-wise. I even started stand-up paddleboarding this summer, and work for a company hosting SUP socials every week.

My advice to other runners struggling through illness is to keep on running. My neurologist always tells me that exercise equals a healthy brain! Try to be optimistic about your disease and take matters into your own hands by reaching for goals that almost seem impossible. I hope this message lets others with RRMS know that a normal healthy and active life is totally possible after diagnosis. You really need to have a positive attitude about it and not let the negative suck you in!

I'd like to share one other little tidbit. I had the opportunity to meet Josh Harding, a goalie for the Minnesota Wild, at a golf tournament a couple years ago. Josh has also been diagnosed with MS. We chatted a bit about the MS foundation he started (Harding's Hope) as well as his being an athlete, living with MS. Fast-forward a year, and someone from my office saw him at an event. He was asking how I was doing, and the staff member mentioned I was training for a full marathon. He sent me a signed photo, and I now keep it on my desk at work as encouragement to get out there and run when I don't feel like it!

A NEW YORK DREAM RIPPED
AWAY FROM HER HEART
DIANE'S STORY

A runner's worst nightmare is an injury that shuts you down.

I went to bed one Friday night with solid plans for a long run the next morning. Through the night I felt this really bad pain, one I had never had. I got up and canceled our planned run and took it easy for the day with plans to head out for a run on Sunday morning instead. That night the pain was all the way down my leg, and it was a pain I had never felt before. It took ten weeks, but after an MRI, I now know I have a bulging disk that is sitting on my S1 nerve.

Through the initial stages, I was told it was a nerve impingement, and I would be running in no time. I would count the days, and was doing all the treatments. I even tried running a few times through the severe pain. But as each week passed, my despair grew deeper and deeper. I stopped talking to friends, and I became a bear to live with, snapping at my husband. Didn't anyone understand that running was my life . . . my soul . . . my everything! I was grieving like someone had died, and to be honest, I probably still am.

No one seems to understand how I feel. No one can relate. I had to cancel the New York Marathon last week. I trained so hard to qualify for New York last year and ran my best marathon time to date at the Niagara Falls International Marathon. Losing New York is heartbreaking. I wake up with an actual pain in my heart each day.

I was very mad at my husband at first. You see, he has had cancer, and I was the only caregiver. When I was first injured, he was so sick that I still had to do everything in the house and drive everywhere. He didn't even notice me as I was lying in pain. After he was better, he still had this *me-me* attitude. I was like, "Oh my God, I can't run . . . can't you see me . . . see my pain?"

The strangest thing is every morning now when I wake up, I don't even know what day it is. Before, every day was marked with a run— a long run, a tempo or speed run, or a recovery workout. Now it's just another day to get through.

I sit here crying as I write this. Things are definitely better twelve weeks in, and I try to grasp at hope most days. I paint a fake smile on face, and I am no longer mad at my husband. I move through each day doing everything in my power to recover.

THE FAITH TO MOVE MOUNTAINS
STEPHANIE'S STORY

I am a single mother and runner from the state of Georgia. And running isn't something that has come easy to my life.

At the age of fourteen, after an automobile accident, I spent two months of my life in a coma on life support. I experienced a traumatic brain injury and lung injury, and I wasn't expected to live. However, with faith, strength, and determination, I did pull through this state—waking to a realization that I was bound to a wheelchair and could not walk. I was told I would be leaving that hospital a handicapped child. There was no hope of me ever walking again.

I recall the day so vividly in my mind . . . I woke up and knew who and where I was, and I have recalled that day every day since 1993. Sitting in front of the nurses' station with my head hanging down and spit rolling uncontrollably out of my mouth, I slowly lifted my head and glanced around and realized I was sitting in a wheelchair. I remember asking myself, *What are you doing, girl, sitting here*, so I said then and there that I was getting up. I tried just that, and fell straight to the floor, realizing I could no longer walk.

That day on my knees on the hospital floor, I made a promise to myself that I could and I would walk out of that hospital no matter what I was being told. And I kept that promise because the same faith, strength, and determination that got me out of that coma eventually walked me out of those hospital doors on October 8, 1993.

Today I say that same faith, strength, and determination have been a bond to my life. They have assisted me through many struggles. They picked me up from the floor of that hospital, led me out those doors, and they have carried me as far as the Boston Marathon finish line.

Twenty-two years after my accident, I give back by sharing the strength I cultivated from those hard moments through a nonprofit brain trauma organization I have developed on my own called Share Your Strong. Speaking with children and individuals worldwide, providing encouragement to stay the course and keep faith so strong you can stand on it. I do this all through my testimony to the power of never giving up in life. I do this because I know for certain we are capable of moving mountains, and I know this because I have moved quite a few, and I am far from done yet . . .

I am Stephanie, a mother, a runner, but most important a survivor . . . Never Give Up, Never Give In, Never Stop Trying, Never *Ever* Give Up!

PUT UP AN OBSTACLE, AND I'LL RUN THROUGH IT
CAROLYN'S STORY

Shortly after running my half-marathon PB, I was diagnosed with aggressive stage 3 breast cancer. I had a single mastectomy, followed by chemotherapy, radiation, and ongoing drug therapy for a year to address the type of cancer I had. A couple of years later, I started the process of reconstruction, which was quite extensive for me, as I didn't have the requisite amount of belly fat to create a breast as most people normally do! Not such a bad problem I guess, but it required several surgeries. Today I am cancer-free.

In the years that followed, I have gone through being diagnosed with ulcerative colitis and suffered through a brutal flare-up, which ended in hospitalization, transfusions, and steroid therapy. I have lived through the death of my beloved father and, most recently, the end of my marriage of twenty-seven years.

Throughout all of this, I have trained and run, mostly without stopping. I have slowed down, and yes, I have taken a few breaks when I absolutely had to. I have had the most incredible support from my coach, who never stopped requiring the work from me, but in a completely manageable way; from my running teammates, who were the most supportive people I can imagine—fast and slow; and from the community as a whole.

I eventually ran Boston, and when I did, I had an incredible posse of people there with me, running with me and supporting me. They knew how hard I'd worked to get there and how much it meant to me. I cried a lot at the finish line that day. I should probably add that my cancer diagnosis came in the fall of 2007, and I was supposed to run Boston in April the following year. Although I wanted to run it, my chemotherapy treatment was aggressive, so I couldn't do it.

Sadly, I had to defer to 2009. But as luck would have it, in the fall of 2008, likely as a result of the chemo, I sustained a stress fracture in my tibia and was told that I couldn't run Boston unless I wanted to risk a complete fracture and the threat of never being able to run again. I was devastated. I asked the BAA (Boston Athletic Association) if I could defer my entry again, and they told me no, their policy was one deferral only. I would have to requalify, so that's exactly what I decided to do. But in the interim, my coach and I wrote emails detailing the situation. Shortly before I was to run the Memphis Marathon in an effort to requalify, I heard from the BAA, telling me that my situation was unique, and that they would let me defer to 2010, and that was the year I eventually lined up for the start of the Boston Marathon. I believe this is just another example of the running community—the heart of the BAA is that of a true runner—encouraging, supportive, and kind. I'm tearing up as I write this . . . it is still very close to my heart.

My running family supports me when I am weak and encourages me when I doubt myself, but most of all, they don't put up with any shit. They require me to be the best I can, and they believe that I can be better than I think I can. I am so grateful for running and my running tribe. They have changed my life enormously, and I cannot imagine my life without them. Today, I am happy and healthy, and running strong.

SHIN SPLINTS, SHAMMY PANTS, AND A BIRDCAGE
CLAIRE'S STORY

I am a runner, or I was a runner until about three weeks ago when I got struck down by the dreaded shin splints. Okay, if I am honest,

I was struck down by it more than three weeks ago, but like any perfectly sane and self-respecting runner I decided to run through the pain. Needless to say, I did more damage, so I had to stop running altogether.

This is right up there with the plague of the locusts for us runners, so before I harmed my nearest and dearest, namely my husband and very tolerant children, I had to find another way of getting my fix. So although I swore I never would, until I am back on my feet I have joined the "spoke folk." Yes, yes, I am sure you cyclists have a derogatory name for us runners too. I dusted off my father-in-law's bike, which has stood in our garage gathering dust for ages, donned my skimpy running shorts (big mistake), and set off on my first ride. After forty minutes of sitting on the instrument of torture, when I could barely see for the tears of pain in my eyes, I headed back home wondering why on earth this was called a sport as opposed to an instrument of war. But I persevered. A friend gave me a pair of cycling shorts; my brother gave me a "birdcage" to put upside down on my head (another good reason to avoid cycling); and three weeks later, I am quite enjoying it.

There are, however, a few things about which I need to warn other unsuspecting runners who turn to cycling. Beware of going so slowly up a steep hill that you fall over sideways into the bushes next to the road. Although I have taken many tumbles while running, I have yet to topple over sideways. A direct hit in the eye by a bug is far more painful when cycling than when running due to the speed at which you are going; however, this does not apply when cycling uphill. Do not think you will be featured in *Style* magazine anytime soon, and be prepared to be overtaken by the people you least expect.

Just the other day with the wind in my hair, or anyway at least what was sticking out from under the birdcage, feeling like I was flying down the road thinking *Wow, I really have this cycling thing waxed,* I noticed a flash of orange coming up behind me. Alas, it was not a police car with lights on about to give me a speeding fine, but a car guard in his orange vest cycling to work on his very "not fancy" bike, and no shammy pants in sight.

So . . . I am thinking of taking up bowling until my shin splints heal and I can get back to my beloved running again.

I COULDN'T BELIEVE I FELT SORRY FOR MYSELF
ADRIANA'S STORY

When I was ten years old, I was diagnosed with juvenile arthritis. The illness took its greatest toll on my two knees. Twice a year my knees were so swollen with synovial fluid that they would become painful and disabling. The doctor usually relieved some of the liquid from my knee with a syringe, and gave me a cortisone injection.

But the years passed, and I got married and had two children. My husband liked to run short distances, and he eventually decided to run a half marathon in the beautiful city of Mazatlan, Mexico. It was his first half marathon, so his father, my mother, my children, and I went to cheer him on. I had never experienced a competition on that scale; I could barely contain my excitement. As the race drew near, we started singing the national anthem, followed by the theme song from the movie *Rocky.* I stood there covered in goose bumps, and when the sound of the official start rang out, I felt as though my world had completely turned upside down. I saw people running with crutches, people in wheelchairs, and visually impaired runners. I started crying—I couldn't believe that I had been feeling sorry for myself.

When my husband finished, I told him that I wanted to run the race next year. So that's what I did. I started training. I could barely run one kilometer, but with my husband's help and motivation, I continued my training. Time passed, and after one year, I didn't just run a half marathon, I participated in the full marathon—my first marathon and my husband's too!

Shortly after that day, I went to see my doctor. He noticed something different in me; who knows, maybe my happiness. He asked me about changes in my life, and I told him about the marathon. He couldn't believe it!

I haven't had problems in my knees since then, and in the years that followed, I have run five marathons and some half marathons. This is my success story, and the story will continue!

CANCER AND THE GUIDANCE OF PATIENCE
ANTHONY'S STORY

I've always run for a reason, although most times I didn't know the true one. But now I have purpose before a run, and anticipate that after-run feeling, knowing it is a calmer, gentler place to be.

Being off for five months with my cancer diagnosis has been my longest forced layoff since I started running. Patience was definitely the key as I began my comeback from the initial treatments. Every run felt like a blessing, and as the duration of the runs increased, I found I had more confidence in the patient approach. I've learned I do indeed possess this trait, and that I was surprisingly comfortable with the whole process of a comeback. Learning I can take the patient methodical approach will help in all facets of life, and especially with phase two of my treatments, which will require a lengthier period of convalescence.

Running has made me feel more resilient in life generally through the improved fitness, last year's diagnosis notwithstanding. If I can make calmer, more rational decisions after a run, then it is feasible I can be a calmer person in general and make better decisions on a wholesale basis.

The running community and social media can make one still feel connected during long periods of injury or illness. I have not had too much contact with fellow runners early in my recuperation, but as I get closer to activity, I find myself more willing to reach out and share my comeback—and in return feel the support and love of friends and fellow runners alike.

LEARNING TO ROLL WITH THE PUNCHES
CHARLOTTE'S STORY

My first race experience was seventy-one days post-surgery for gall-stones, and the removal of my gallbladder. I worked through it one day at a time by increasing both distance and the time I was out, block by block. It made me realize that bouncing back after surgery was a gradual process. I set a race as a goal in mid-September, almost a month after surgery. I learned to roll with the punches and that stub-bornness can work in your favor if you just let it be. It was extreme focus that got me to my first start line, and helped me finish that race.

Along my running journey, I was diagnosed with anxiety and de-pression, and it hasn't been easy. Running isn't the whole me, but it makes me whole. Running gives me one more outlet to heal and dis-cover that I am enough. It also reminds me I'm worthy of being part of a great sport and community. I've been able to take on the men-tor/cheerleader role. Even though I was in almost last place, a friend of mine was glad I was cheering her on and that I was able to walk behind her toward the finish area. I'm honored to help others, and through injury and illness, I've built an optimistic outlook that I'm glad to share.

A RUNNER REBORN AS A TRIATHLETE
SANDIE'S STORY

My running (athletic) life has been reborn after a long deterioration of my hip joint to osteoarthritis. When I was told that a total hip replacement was a certainty when it got bad enough, and perhaps I should stop running to preserve the joint for as long as possible—my lifeline was yanked *hard*. Trying to observe that advice presented me with the opportunity to learn about how we behave when we have adopted a label, and how our choice to tear off that label and behave differently is a matter of free will. Eventually, a wiser surgeon, who saw me as a runner with a hip problem, told me that it was a matter of carpentry for him, and as long as I could suck up the pain, I might as well do what I needed to do. That gave me five more years of running, and prompted me to take up cycling so that I could keep doing the big distances that gave me so much inner space for meditation.

My last Sunday run with my tribe was a walk around the block with my cane in December 2013. In January 2014, I had a total hip replacement. By April, I was back on my bike and learning to power walk. Later in June, I completed my fourth Ride to Conquer Cancer double-century ride, and with my run tribe, I was doing one and tens—run one, walk ten . . . instead of the other way around! In January 2015, I started swimming, and this summer I completed two triathlons, and I am well on my way to being competitive in my age group.

My advice for injured runners is to understand what's holding you back, and why. Is it really just physical, or is it a life lesson? Accept it for what it is, and welcome the opportunity to learn. Then do the work to get through it. What you find on the other side will be worth the effort.

A NIGGLE, A PAIN, AND THE LESSON WITHIN
MICHELLE'S STORY

Over the years, I have been sidelined by injury, illness, not to mention life circumstances. I suffer from chronic bronchitis and have had many bouts that have pulled me off running for an entire winter season. The list of running injuries is much too long to list, but every runner has their Achilles' heal—pun intended. Mine is my calves. So many times right before a race I would end up with a calf tear. There is nothing more frustrating for a runner than to work for an entire season only to get sidelined weeks before the big dance.

The first couple of times were hard for me to deal with. I can admit I made people's lives around me miserable. I was quite literally addicted to running, so not running was inconceivable. I had to take extreme measures to get better at dealing with my injuries. After you go through it a few times, you learn that injury is part of the game of running.

It's not about *if* you will get injured but *when.* That was my first lesson. The second was learning to understand what was a niggle and what was pain. Listening to your body is the most important tool you can sharpen. The one and most valuable lesson I learned through all these years of running is that "Rest Is Best." It sounds cliché and simple, but it's absolutely true. Taking a day off only to go out and do a workout on an injury the next day will only prolong your injury. Stringing as many days off together and focusing on rehab rather than running will promote healing, and in my experience makes you a stronger runner. It's a fact that many elite runners have run their best races coming off an injury. It was the forced rest and period of rehab that got them to the race, and gave them the energy to push harder.

Training for a race closely mimics life. You set a goal, and you have to do A, B, and C to achieve that goal. In life, you want that job promotion. You have to put in the hours, the hard work, and the commitment. The same is true for running. You have to commit. In terms of being more resilient in life, I'm much calmer and less frantic or angry when things don't go as planned. I take things in stride (again pun intended). I've learned through my training that every day will be different, and every day will bring new challenges and surprises.

In life, I can't expect every day to go perfectly. In the past, I would have struggled with the loss of control when things went sideways on me. Now I accept it and deal with the things I can and let the rest take care of itself. Much like healing from an injury, you can only do so much, and time will have to take care of the rest.

THE SPEED BUMPS WE MEET ALONG THE WAY
JACQUELINE'S STORY

Over the last year, since upping my mileage for half-marathon and marathon training, I've "run into" numerous problems with runner's knee and plantar fasciitis. It's never been anything more serious than anything rest and visits to the physiotherapist and massage therapist can handle, but enough to put speed bumps into my training calendar.

I was diagnosed with anxiety and depression in university; although I manage it pretty well now, I still have "those days" where the last thing I want to do is be physically active, and I don't want to see anyone or do anything. This life circumstance occasionally side-lines me from sticking with my planned training schedule.

Throughout it all, I've learned that it's okay to not be okay—whether it's physically or emotionally, we're all entitled to those off days. I've always had a go-getter attitude and approach to everything I do, and with these speed bumps, I've had to learn to say no and accept that it's more than okay to take time off.

Although these experiences may have sidelined me temporarily, with each speed bump, I find myself bouncing back stronger than the last. In dealing with my anxiety, I know that my off days will only last as long as I let them, and keeping that mind-set when these adversities come helps me fight them head-on.

Connecting with other runners and following others' experiences on social media has shown me that my experiences aren't necessarily unique to me. Everyone hits a wall, everyone has hurdles to get over, but how we handle those adversities is what defines us. I love being able to reach out to other runners through social media for advice on getting over these speed bumps and seeing how other people handle their different situations. It has made me a more open-minded person and helped me be more aware of what my running practice needs.

TAKING THE TIME TO MOVE INTO
A MORE JOYOUS LIFE
SHERRY'S STORY

I have a day job, but I am also the owner of Busy Zen Life, where I demonstrate to people that you can beat your anxiety and be happy and healthy by moving, breathing, doing yoga, meditating, and committing to living a beautiful life. I am always running toward a stronger, better, healthier, happier me, and I am also often trying to outrun stress and anxiety. So far, both are working!

What has changed the most is that this year I am not training for anything, so I am really running just for the sheer joy of it. I always loved running, but having the freedom to decide to run just because I want to run is very different. If I have a bad day at work or I'm feeling more anxious than usual, I can just go out and run for as long as it takes for me to feel better without worrying about things like, *Okay I have to run X miles today to be ready for my next race.* It's been good for reminding me that running isn't just a goal; it's a life choice.

I have specifically chosen to avoid anxiety treatments in the pharmaceutical sense. I am not against antidepressants or anti-anxiety meds, but I choose not to take them at this time simply because I am sensitive to medicinal side effects, and almost all the most common side effects for those specific meds are the same things I already experience when I have anxiety. Running, yoga, and meditation have helped me so much with my anxiety without all the scary side effects. I've always said that if the big pharma companies could actually legitimately bottle the runner's high, they would make a killing—but they can't, so I chase it the authentic way.

Last year I ran my very first half marathon. There was a time when I struggled to run five kilometers, so if you had told me that I'd one day run twenty-one kilometers, I would have laughed. So how has this made me more resilient? Some days when I'm struggling to do something in my daily life, whether it's a tough work task or breathing through an anxiety attack, I can say to myself, *For the love of God, woman, you ran a half marathon. If you can do that, you can get through this day!*

I was diagnosed with vertigo back in December. Because of the intense dizziness on a near-constant level, I was unable to run when I normally would have started training for this year's race season. I ended up not even being able to race at all. I was actually really depressed and terrified that I would never be able to run again. Luckily, I became friends with an excellent chiropractor who told me she believed my vertigo was caused by compression in my neck. She started treating me, and basically saved my life. She got me back on my feet—literally—and back out on the road.

The day that I finally ran ten kilometers again was a very emotional day for me. What I would tell other runners who are sidelined is to find someone who can help you. Someone who not only believes in you but also understands runners. If your doctor is telling you that you can't run anymore, find someone else who has helped runners and gets the draw and addiction to running.

FINDING INSPIRATION AND MOTIVATION IN YOUR GREATEST FEAR
ROBYN'S STORY

I run for therapy. I run for time to think without anyone around. I run to sort out my thoughts. I run to feel strong. I've never really considered myself an athlete, so I also run to prove I'm capable of getting faster. I'm running toward a healthier me. I'm running toward a me who loves myself in my entirety and is proud of what I can accomplish. I'm running away from the possibility of never being able to run someday.

I called off my wedding in 2012 and left a very toxic relationship. Before then, I had only really done one 5K and one 10K race. I started running (again) to battle depression and anxiety, and I later joined a run club to get out of the house and be around like-minded people who were looking to stay committed to a weekly run practice.

I didn't know I was treating myself with the runner's high, but it was the combination of physical fitness, getting a runner's high, and being around amazing individuals that helped me on my healing journey from the heartbreak.

My running practice has evolved to dealing with injuries and ensuring I'm strengthening everything. For example, I'll always ensure I'm doing side glute exercises when I'm in the gym for leg day so that I can avoid ITB pain. I'm now dealing with an ankle injury, so I've purchased a foam pad for balance exercises to strengthen my ankle stabilizers.

I'm dealing with a bruised ankle (talus) bone at the moment. I sprained my ankle in September 2014, and then ran an OCR the next weekend on it. I must've dislodged my anklebone, as I lost most mobility in my left foot and couldn't flex it up (dorsiflex). Later that December, I was diagnosed with MS (multiple sclerosis), so I never really dealt with my ankle injury.

I find inspiration in knowing that I may not always be able to run, so I run to make my life better now while I still can. One day, I could wake up and my autoimmune disease could progress without warning, and I may not be able to walk, let alone run. So, I run now to be stronger than my diagnosis.

When I started training again in January of this year, I ignored my ankle pain, as I was dealing with my MS. I ignored the pain and basically ran on an impinged ankle for six months before seeing a sports doctor. Now that I'm working on mobility, I'm resting my ankle during the week. I'm not training, and just racing with my ankle taped. For it to truly heal, I need to take a full six to twelve weeks off, but I've got so many races! So now my goal is to not injure myself more and just survive the races. My advice is: Don't do what I've done. Deal with pain immediately. Do your rehab and strengthening exercises and rest fully! Easier said than done.

My other advice when dealing with illness or life circumstances is to run your run. You don't need to be as fast as John Smith. You just need to do it for yourself. No matter how slow you run, you are still a runner. I was never fast before my diagnosis, but now if I battle symptoms during a run, I slow down. It can feel like I'm running in mud, and my limbs get so heavy. I want to inspire others to call themselves runners no matter what distance they conquer or how fast they are. If you run, you are still a runner and should be so proud of that.

Running has helped me find how to control and find my inner happiness. When I'm active, fit, and tackling new goals like running different races, I have purpose. I cross off a goal, and I'm accomplished and ready for the next challenge. I treat runs, workouts, and races as short-term goals that are just checklist items on the happiness journey of accomplishment.

GIVING MYSELF PERMISSION TO BE ANGRY, UPSET, AND DISAPPOINTED
EMILY'S STORY

I currently am on a permanent sideline with an inoperable ganglion cyst on my soleus, a partially torn meniscus, and PES bursitis. I feel like I'm still working through the process because it's quite a recent diagnosis. I'm learning something new about myself every day, and they aren't always good things.

It's an incredibly ugly side of me that's come out. I don't like to be told I can't do something, and I like it even less when it's something I used to be able to do. I've watched friends, training partners, and other runners beat personal bests, beat *my* personal bests, and generally get to keep living their running lives normally, while I'm in pain and unable to run.

The vast depths of my jealousy have been epic and unnerving. It's been really hard to be happy for people as they conquer their first, seventh, or best marathons, and I feel awful admitting that. It's almost like I don't know who I am without being able to do the things I enjoy, and I have to relearn who I am without distance running.

At first, I did a lot of eating and feeling sorry for myself. The diagnostic process was long, and I'm usually in some form of pain, and I definitely used that as a vessel for pity. But more recently, I'm starting to focus on shorter distances (I'm allowed to do 5K occasionally), lifting, and using cycling for my endurance activities. I'm definitely feeling the fog start to lift.

I've always been a resilient person, and a firm believer that it's not what happens to you, but how you handle it—not that it makes struggle any easier. I feel almost like it isn't in me to just give up; that no matter what, I'll come out of any situation (maybe only a little bit scarred).

Being emotionally resilient and physically resilient are two different beasts, though. And I feel like my physical resilience hasn't been tested like this since my epilepsy diagnosis when I was fifteen years old. Being forced to slow down physically is making me face a lot of my emotional demons that tend to just get worked out when you spend a few good hours running. Giving myself permission to be angry, upset, and disappointed about my injury, instead of just pretending that I'm okay with it and powering right along, has been a big game changer and something I'll take with me for my next challenge. Allowing yourself to go through it and experience all of your feelings is life altering.

A FRACTURED FOOT, A NEWBORN,
AND THE HEALING OF TIME
JENNIFER'S STORY

In March 2011, while I was teaching some agility moves for a "Body Attack" at a fitness club in Halifax, I rolled over on my foot, heard a snap, and went down. Class was over. The club manager and some trainers got me to the manager's car and took me to the hospital. With a fracture in my foot, I knew I would be sidelined for a while with both my running and teaching of fitness classes.

While an injury at any time can be depressing, this was eight weeks before I returned to work after my second child. I was stuck at home with a seven-month-old and had a four-year-old in day care during the day. I had to transport my infant upstairs to his crib many times a day, and was relying on crutches as I dropped off and picked up my older son at a day care. To make matters worse, I had to climb two flights of stairs to get to his classroom.

I had completed the Hypothermic Half Marathon mere weeks before, and was trying to keep up longer weekend runs to maintain fitness so I would be able to run the Bluenose Marathon in May. Having to give up my midweek and long Sunday runs was painful. Running and teaching fitness classes were my coping mechanisms for my limited patience in dealing with young children. It was also how I coped with the stress of preparing to return to a busy work life.

I tried pool running, but I felt it challenging not to use my foot. To add insult to injury, while running laps at Dalhousie University's sports complex, I was heckled by two 13-year-old boys because I was running in the water. I felt deflated; I was quickly gaining weight with weaning off nursing and barely any physical activity. I learned that I didn't have a strong coping mechanism. I was unhappy, and I am sure I was unpleasant to be around.

This experience has helped me realize that most injuries will have a finite recovery period despite how hard it is to see and believe when you're in the recovery period. Since that injury, I have badly sprained my ankle, and then developed a Morton's neuroma. These injuries have forced me to withdraw, defer races, or reduce distances. I have reminded myself that if I take my time and let my body recover, it will heal faster, and I will have time to achieve my goals. I will lose any weight I put on. It is not over. Injuries, age . . . they really don't matter in the end. I will keep running.

I KEEP THINKING WHAT I COULD
HAVE DONE DIFFERENTLY
ROSE'S STORY

Author's note: Three days ago, I was out on my fifty-five-kilometer (thirty-four-mile) Sunday long run, and as is typically the case, my buddy Almis joined up with me for part of the run. We had just passed the downtown core and were heading out into a rather desolate industrial section of the running trail. As we neared the little drawbridge, we saw a group of runners standing around talking to some police officers who were patrolling the area on their bikes. We waved as we ran past, and that's when one of the runners said, "Hey . . . are you JP? I follow you on Instagram." We stopped and chatted for a bit, and I noticed that one of the runners had blood dripping from her knee. She said she had fallen on the bridge, but she appeared okay. Almis and I continued on for the rest of our run, but later in the day I discovered that the runner had sustained a rather serious injury. I was in the process of wrapping up this injury-and-illness chapter of my book, so I decided to reach out to this young lady and asked if she would feel comfortable sharing how she was feeling emotionally and physically less than twenty-four hours after her injury. Fortunately, Rose was open to the idea, and what follows is, in my mind, one of the most beautifully articulated glimpses inside the mind of an injured runner.

It's Monday, and today is my usual rest day—although sometimes I go for a ride on my bike or I cross-train a little, mainly because I just can't sit still. Running is my antidepressant, and today I can say I honestly have not felt this down in years. I know it's just been a few weeks, but in the last ten weeks I have worked so hard to bring my running to another level, and I felt I was there. I was getting faster, and I was so happy. Last year, I qualified for Boston at the Chicago Marathon with a time of 3:42:59, and I needed 3:55. I'm supposed to run Chicago again in six weeks, and I had set a goal of 3:40. I know I am, or was, capable of reaching it, and not simply to get another Boston qualifier. I've only ever wanted to run Boston once so that it would always be special. I desperately wanted that 3:40 just to prove to myself that I am good at this; finally, something I am good at.

But all that changed yesterday . . . I was out on my long run and heading back toward the downtown core. I had just passed the rest of my friends who stopped to wait for the others in our group. As I came up to the drawbridge, I saw that there were cyclists and people running toward me, so I veered to the right, and that's when my shoe caught part of the metal grate on the bridge platform. I went down really hard on the metal surface of the bridge. I guess I tried to break my fall with my hands, but I still ended up banging my knee. Initially, I was in shock, and I had no idea how serious my fall had been. The result was a fractured wrist and two cracks in my left kneecap.

So here I am today twenty-four hours after my fall, and I feel like

I failed. I keep thinking about what I could have done differently. I had set out on a continuous thirty-kilometer run, with twenty kilometers at race pace. I didn't wait for my friends, or my sister. I just kept running with my own focus. I didn't stop. It wasn't a "fun run" . . . I was training for me, myself, and I. Today I keep thinking if I weren't so selfish and had stopped to wait for them, and taken our usual selfies and water breaks, I wouldn't have fallen.

I'm mad. I'm angry. I'm feeling sorry for myself. I keep crying, and that's just dumb isn't? Deep down I know it's just a bump in the road. I will heal fast, and just like everyone keeps telling me I will come back stronger.

But in my head I think, *What if I don't?* What if my knee injury causes future issues? What if I can't run anymore? What if I get fat? I'm forty-seven. . . I'm not twenty-something! But I keep telling myself to snap out of it! I laugh, and then I start crying again. I know my injuries will heal, and I will run again in a little while. I remind myself that there are far more horrible things going on in the world. But that's the logical me talking, and I'm not feeling logical today. Tomorrow, I will be more positive . . . right?

I fell yesterday at exactly seventeen kilometers . . . not a word of a lie, the first thing I did while I was still on the ground was stop my Garmin.

A MEMORY OF THE PAST AND A HOPE FOR THE FUTURE
JENNIFER'S STORY

When I recall the day it happened, it all comes back to me so clearly. It was nearly nine o'clock, and I was almost late for work.

The sky was perfectly blue with not a cloud in sight. For the first week of October in New York, it was the kind of day that needed to be spent outside, not stuck indoors at work; it was the last day that resembled summer.

Seven months earlier my wife and I had gotten married—it was our eighth year together and the right time. We planned our wedding in a week, and it was the perfect day. That April morning I woke up and thought, *I'm getting married today, I'm going for a run.* I laced up my sneakers and headed out. It was a special run—it was my last run as a non-married woman. What a run it was—four miles, barely walked any of it (a major accomplishment at the time), found some roads that took me away from the little village I lived in and near a golf course—major roads and residential, tree-lined streets; it was magical. Whenever I recall my wedding day, I always remember those four glorious miles that seemed nearly effortless, as though they brought me closer to a love I only thought I had known.

Seven months later I thought it would be great to have a date night, so as the sun kissed my cheeks and I walked the three blocks to work, I called my wife to discuss a date night—a concept we never truly embraced because we always found something to do together we enjoyed. Yet I thought a structured night of movies and dinner would be exactly what we needed. I went my usual route, down the main road on the sidewalk, down the hill, and made my way around the dips and grooves in the sidewalk, around the piles of garbage bags on the sidewalk placed out for garbage day.

I crossed the street ahead of me and turned to cross to get to the building that would have me for the next eight hours working; at least it was Friday, and I had date night to look forward to that evening. I waited for the light to change and the walk icon to appear on the traffic signal. I began to walk, crossed halfway to the crosswalk when I felt I was moving faster; I saw the white markings of the crosswalk coming toward my face, I was falling but I could not stop myself. I must have fallen completely to the ground, but immediately stood up. I turned to see a pickup truck stopped behind me. I looked around—my glasses had fallen off my face, my handbag off my shoulder, my flip-flop from my foot, and my cell phone from my hand. My arms went up as I yelled to the front of the truck "You hit me . . . You hit me." I said it slowly and in total disbelief. I turned to figure out all that had occurred while all the while, the blue sky overhead and the sun just began to blur, and the realization that there was pain in my body began.

An ambulance ride to the emergency room, diagnostic testing, an injection of medication, a prescription of pills, family and friends rushing to my bedside, and then I was released to go home.

As I returned home, the sky was still blue and the sun was still shining. I took the stairs one leg at a time and found my way to the couch. My eyelids became heavy, and I slept.

In the weeks that followed, I learned that the fractures in my back required passive treatment and time to heal. It took more than two months to return to work. It took three months for the anxiety to kick in. It took four months to stop taking muscle relaxers. It took six months to realize I did not need to take antidepressants. It took nearly a year to realize I feared crossing the street—any street.

It took a year and a half to not experience any physical pain. It took two years to be able to reflect on all that happened and know I survived. There is a but . . .

But I cannot run anymore. I have tried. I go for walks and will try to run a few yards—at one point, the pain was immediate; then the pain came hours later; more recently, the pain arrives two days later with a vengeance. That last episode led me to a dose of a muscle relaxer, as over-the-counter medication would not lessen the pain, pain I had not experienced in many months.

Two steps forward, three steps back. Two steps forward, three steps back! Two steps forward, three steps back?

I had a blog. The blog was about being a slow runner, being the last to finish a race, a back-of-the-pack plodder who would not hesitate to walk mid-race. I trained for half marathons and participated in large New York Road Runner races and more local, small-town races. 5K, 15K, half marathon—they were all so enjoyable. I blogged about my training and running: before work, after work, in the rain, in the heat, watching seasoned and very fit runners pass me on the sidewalks in my town, feeling despair that I was slow, and then thriving on the fact that I was out there among those seasoned runners. Those runners did not judge me by my speed or my appearance. They passed me and smiled. They hollered affirmations to me in races. They cheered as I crossed the finish line.

The blog was deleted long before the back injury and with that, the Twitter account that accompanied it. I had been feeling exposed, and I put that part of me to rest with the stories I had composed. The running continued, though. The morning runs, the weekend long runs, and the last half marathon I completed with a time that had impressed even me. My social media presence is less pronounced now, and what I share even more contained. My running is a memory of the past and a hope for the future.

The daily pain is gone, but the reminders are more than skin-deep. I have gained weight, but not in the vain, stereotypical way women often complain about. Running was helpful in keeping my muscles toned, my lungs and mind clear, my legs strong, and my posture regal. I cared less about the food I ate and instead about how it would sustain me through a run or better prepare me for the training I was participating in at the time.

More recently, I have had these realizations, and I have had more time to sit and think of the things I *can* change rather than waiting for things to get better, for my running to magically return to me. The reality is that it may never return to me, that walking may need to be enough, that other activities and low-impact, non-aggressive exercise may be the key to my success. But it's not what I want. I want to have the morning I trained for—my wedding morning—back again. I want to feel the effortlessness of a good run. I want to hear strangers cheering for me, I want to make new friends who will laugh about how sweaty and stinky we have become and commiserate about the special laundry detergents we have to use, not for our delicates, but rather our running tights. There is another but . . .

But that is not today's reality.

Today, I do not run. Today, I do not commiserate with anyone from the running community. When I bought a new pair of running sneakers in the hope of running again, my buddy at the running store cocked his head to the side and said, "You need a new doctor, one who will let you run."

But it's not about the doctor—it's about the pain. And the pain proves the doctor right, each time. I did not require surgery from this accident; I also plan to not require surgery in the future because of pushing my body after the injuries I sustained.

But . . . today I am healthy, my bones and body are intact. My worst days nowadays usually involve me cringing when watching other people cross the street. Yes, sometimes I fear such for myself, but I always cross safely. I no longer have flashbacks of the accident, and I have forgiven many people along the way.

My running experience has helped. In a way, the lessons I learned from running—the perseverance, the drive, the training, and the continuous return on investment of energy put in to the sport, physical and mental—have taught me what I needed to know to survive this experience.

If I never run again, I have learned that life parallels the way I trained: Not every day, as with every run, is going to be good. Some days, like some runs, are going to feel endless and painful, while others will feel graceful and effortless. I have learned that as I work through things, be it crossing the street or training for a half marathon, when I set attainable goals, they can be achieved.

These are the words that I can share about the way running has enhanced and affected my life. These are the comparisons and memories that leave my eyes full of tears as I reflect on all that has occurred. Running made me strong physically and mentally, so to have the option of running taken away from me in the blink of an eye is like losing a friend, a close and dear friend. Words cannot fully capture all that the sport has done to enhance my life. My heart tells me I am still a runner, but my body questions that often.

My life looks different now compared with a few years ago. I'm sure that two years from now, things will look different as well. Who knows, maybe running will be a part of my life in the future, maybe it won't be, or perhaps another athletic community will find their way into my heart. One way or another, I plan to cherish my running memories and use them to fuel my journey along the training route we call life.

Building Your Tribe

If you want to travel fast, go alone.
If you want to travel far, go together.
—African proverb

The Pakistani writer Mohsin Hamid once said: "Empathy is about finding echoes of another person in yourself." I couldn't agree more, yet I would go even further by suggesting that resonating in those echoes is the real connection we all seek—that intangible bond that is nowhere as apparent as in the international running community. How else could you account for the incredible support, the blossoming friendships, and the heartfelt empathy that have come to characterize a seemingly disparate group of individuals not only online but also on the roads and trails that connect us?

We live in a highly charged, chaotic world—one in which our brains are wired to constantly seek meaning in the randomness all around us. The German neurologist Klaus Conrad coined the word *apophenia* to describe the innate human desire to seek meaning and patterns in the meaningless. In fact, by examining free associations as trapdoors into our psyche, the branch of psychology known as psychoanalysis deals in the realm of that subtle hand of apophenia. It's ironic that as our mind attempts to connect the dots of disorder all around us, we grasp at people who cross our path as a means to build intrepid bridges of connection through the minefield of disorder.

I think we can all agree that the busier our lives get, the more difficult it is to carve out the space to simply breathe and recharge, let alone the time to do what lights us up. Increasingly, we are stepping away from the frenetic pace around us by isolating, and for many of us this means vegging out in front of our screens. Sadly, instead of reducing our stress and replenishing our energy, our new default coping strategy might be making the problem worse.

In his book *Spark: The Revolutionary New Science of Exercise and the Brain*, John J. Ratey points out: "A common protocol scientists use to induce the physiological stress response in rats is to remove them from their social structure; simply isolating them activates stress hormones. The same is true in humans: It's stressful to be shunned or isolated. Loneliness is a threat to survival. Not coincidentally, the less physically active we are, the less likely we'll be to reach out and touch someone." Ratey goes on, "Studies show that by adding physical activity to our lives, we become more socially active—it boosts our confidence and provides an opportunity to meet people" (page 70). What Ratey is referring to is a chemical response that closely mimics what happens in our brain when we introduce a moderate infusion of drugs or alcohol, but with one notable difference: Social engagement offers far more lasting effects on our overall well-being.

And that brings me to another point. For as long as I can remember, I've been attracted to the margins—those places inhabited by the wanderers, the disenfranchised, and more recently the addicted. Growing up as a survivor of childhood trauma, I became adept at revealing just enough of myself to fit into whatever community I desperately wanted to be a part of. Living life as an emotional chameleon, I had built bridges to others that were forged entirely out of superficial or inauthentic relationships. Sure, from a distance, I appeared to be sliding through my life on a socially connected high, but deep down inside all I felt was uncoiled and detached.

Much of our identity is determined by our interactions with the broader community, so is not surprising that by subverting our true identity simply to satisfy our thirst for belonging, we inadvertently sabotage any chance of forming actual or meaningful connections. From my own experience, I can attest to how exhausting all this can be, and how more often than not, it is a fast track to depression, anxiety, and further isolation. We often hear that "It takes a village to raise a child," yet we are quick to dismiss the importance of that village once this child becomes an adult. The remarkable discovery that I made through running, and one with which the other contributors to this book would concur, is that whether or not we realized it at the time, most of us began running as a means to unlock something primal inside us—and the key to unlocking that thing is the sense of community and belonging that running brings into our lives.

When I speak of community, I am not using the term in the colloquial sense of "neighborhood"; I'm referring to the feeling of belonging we receive through mutual identification at a deeper level with like-minded individuals. The danger of any community is that by its very nature, it can be prone to elitism and exclusion. In my mind, real community exists when individual differences are seen as gifts, and thus each is worthy of being brought to light.

Before going into the importance of building your tribe among the running community, I thought I should at least touch upon the teachings of Jean Vanier, the founder of L'Arche. Founded in 1964, L'Arche is now an international federation dedicated to creating communities of caregivers and volunteers who work with, and live alongside, people with developmental disabilities. In Canada alone, there are nearly two hundred such settings. In the beautiful words of Jean Vanier, "One of the marvelous things about community is that it enables us to welcome and help people in a way we couldn't as individuals. When we pool our strength and share the work and responsibility, we can welcome many people, even those in deep distress, and perhaps help them find self-confidence and inner healing."

In reading through the hundreds of stories that those of you in the running community submitted for this book, I was able to distill three common characteristics, or threads, that many runners use to describe what they are looking for within their running tribe.

GRAVITATION TOWARD GROWTH

Running does not require that we run in groups, yet there appears to be something primal within runners that draws us, and in some respects compels us, to seek out the company of other runners. Whether we pursue this pack mentality in person or online, the attraction of joining a broader running community is rooted in our belief that through building a tribe, we can take advantage of reciprocal personal growth, something that is either impossible or at least difficult to achieve on our own.

It was also clear from my interviews that the running community is predicated on an overriding degree of inclusion, one that sees beyond cultural, social, and athletic differences. Groups may in fact comprise a group leader and many followers, but this distinction appears to be fluid, as group members invariably take on many roles throughout their participation. Based on my own experience, with the exception of a coach or trainer, the leader of a running group could more accurately be described as an attractor—someone who has the capacity to inspire, motivate, and encourage those around him or her to be more complete athletes. As Shawn pointed out in his interview with me, there are "those who can lead today and follow tomorrow. We are all led by those who inspire us, and there is no shortage of inspiring feats within a running group." He goes on to say, "As a new member to the running community, I try to learn and be inspired by the veteran runner who has completed his or her hundredth marathon. I strive to run faster, like the 1:12 half marathoner, and I want to build my endurance like the ultramarathoner who runs a hundred miles. These people all lead in their own way, either by coaching others in the community, by providing encouragement, or simply by being a positive example of how to achieve your individual goals."

By aligning ourselves with a running group or by amassing our own online running tribe, we tap into one critical advantage that we cannot access on our own—accountability. I know when I first moved up from the half-marathon distance to the marathon, the prospect of heading out alone on a bitterly cold Sunday morning in January for a three-hour run was not only daunting, but enough to make me want to bury my head under the covers and stay nestled in my cozy bed. Some mornings, simply knowing that there were five of my running mates waiting for me out on the dark street corner was the only thing motivating me to get up and get it done. Accountability is also a key driver in many of the social media interactions between runners. Reading a post about another runner's mileage or race result may inspire you or intimidate you, but in either case it can be the fuel to ignite your own running passion.

The runners I surveyed also expressed the competitive or athletic edge that group participation brings to their running practice. Anyone who has ever put in a serious and sustained tempo run knows how much easier it is to push yourself when you are engaged in a group tempo run. When I look over at the face of another runner who is obviously in distress and pushing his or her tempo limits, it reminds me that what I'm doing is indeed challenging, and more often than not everyone on that tempo run will slip in and out of periods of discomfort throughout the run. Another benefit of becoming a member of a running community, and one that I believe is even more enriching online, is the ability to take advantage of the group's cumulative knowledge in terms of sports nutrition, training regimens, injury advice, and race preparation.

The most rewarding running groups are those that have a tacit understanding for the need for space to allow individuals and the group itself time to reflect, rejuvenate, and grow. This feature is most typically exhibited by the absence of pressure to perform at a certain or prescribed level. Each individual thus determines excellence, and the metric for the club's or the online community's excellence is based solely upon the cumulative joy that comes with participation or identification with the group.

What we are left with is a feeling of security as we begin to tentatively expand our comfort zone. Again I would turn to the insightful words of Jean Vanier: "To be lonely is to feel unwanted and unloved, and therefore unlovable. Loneliness is a taste of death." Ultimately, our association with the running community teaches us to accommodate and to compromise, both of which are essential skills we must foster if we hope to have any kind of longevity in our sport.

OUR DESIRE TO BUILD BRIDGES AND BONDS

Despite the growing pains we might experience learning to accommodate the broad spectrum of personalities within the running community, there is no denying that exposure to diversity spawns creativity. By far, one of the most dynamic properties of any group organized around one primary function, in our case running, is the unspoken acceptance that there will be a lot of overlap within your community. In addition to our shared passion for running, that is, many of our peripheral interests or activities will overlap with those of others in the group.

And herein lies the unique nature of running, compared with other sports: When we come together to run, particularly as we move toward longer distances in our training, we find ourselves moving alongside other members of the group for what is often hours at a time. I consider the time I devote to running on my own as a non-judgmental space in which I process whatever weighs heavy on me at the time, as well as a calming space whereby through a moving meditation, I can either sit with discomfort or invite joy into my life. Contrasting that are my daily interactions with other runners on social media, combined with the time I devote each week to running with two other men, both of whom have become like family to me over the years. In each instance, because of a mutual love of running, I feel as though our usual defenses are down, and that allows us to move beyond the superficial interactions that we typically engage in throughout the day.

Human behavior is dictated by our innate need to understand how other people feel and our desire to connect with others at a deeper level. I believe that at its best, the running community demonstrates this thirst for connection. I would even venture to add that regardless of your opinion on all the "running selfies" populating your social media streams, our eagerness to share these pictures can be seen as an attempt to encapsulate, or capture, that feeling of community we derive from our running circles. All vanity aside, it's our way of shouting out *Notice me* or *Look at us.* By participating in a sport that is often brutally lonely and isolating at times, runners are desperate to build those bonds, or bridges, to the broader community.

As is society at large, the running community is also subdivided into smaller clusters of shared-interest groups—some might refer to it as tribes within the broader running community. But as we see when we line up for a race, or on a grander scale when the entire running community was grieving after the Boston Marathon bombings, runners quite readily shed their tribal affiliations and come together as one running family.

To my mind, there are two key elements driving our connectivity as a running community. At the micro level, we set out to create bonds with other runners whose interests overlap or in some way align with ours; while at a macro level, we seek to create bridges to other running communities that, for whatever reason, lie outside our zone of reference. And here is where social media has had a significant impact on the sport of running. Case in point: When it comes to building bridges, we tend to do it in a variety of ways such as local groups expanding their reach to include international runners, novice runners seeking advice from veteran and elite runners, or even something as basic as medium-distance runners following the adventures of extreme endurance athletes online in order to get a glimpse into a world that appears so foreign to them.

Heading out for a long run with a big group of runners, or even just one other runner, provides us ample time to share our story and invite someone else into our lives. As one of the contributors to this book told me, we tend to have surprisingly deep conversations when we're out on a run, and that may have something to do with the lack of eye contact or absence of pressure to respond that typifies most of our interactions outside running. As I've mentioned many times, I'm an addict in recovery, so I have lots of experience when it comes to opening up about my fears and feelings; still, with the exception of my 12-step meetings and sessions with my therapist, I don't dig into those core feelings very often. However, I should add that in both cases, that open dialogue is generally forced out of me due to the therapeutic environment, whereas the occasions in which I've shared openly about something personal during a run were, to some degree, more fluid and open.

SEEKING AUTHENTICITY
THROUGH VULNERABILITY

Mark Hyman, the physician and *New York Times* best-selling author, once stated: "Your social networks may matter more than your genetic networks. But if your friends have healthy habits, you are more likely to as well. So get healthy friends." That certainly rings true for me because I've seen time and again that the longer you stick around the running community, the healthier your network of friends becomes. By its very nature, running demands that we adopt a healthy lifestyle, one conducive to lessening the physical demands that running entails. As a recovering addict, I would definitely say that my need to embrace a healthier lifestyle was what initially drew me to running, and eventually to expanding my social network to include other like-minded individuals.

Much has been written about the physical benefits of sustaining a regular running practice, but I believe we tend to discount the socio-psychological importance of being actively engaged in a thriving community—in our case, the community of runners both online and in our run groups. Most of us bounce through life rushing from one family or work commitment to another, and all the while, we feel so hurried that we long for authentic connection, a connection that only comes when we are able to be truly present in the moment. It's as if we are constantly on the lookout for ways to connect with those around us, yet what we fail to recognize is that we are already connected; it's simply a matter of acknowledging and finding those connections. It is through the experience of belonging that we strive to be our best, and despite what we often tell ourselves, it is a process that is really rather simple. As we learn to accommodate those around us, most notably the people in our chosen groups, we grow to define them, and in so doing we define ourselves.

Chances are you were brought up in a society in which children and adolescents engaged in a lot of team sports. And when we look back on that pivotal time in our development, we begin to realize how our physical and social well-being were almost inseparable. There is a good chance that you participated in at least one team sport during those years. But something happens along the way in our transition from adolescence into adulthood—the vast majority of us stop participating in team sports, and instead opt for forms of exercise and physical activity that we can do on our own. And when you think about that, it really is a shame. We lose track of the social aspect, the opportunity for connection that we are desperately seeking as adults. I believe the exponential growth in gym memberships and the spike in registration for boot camps, adventure races, and online fitness programs signal that innate need we have to connect with others in a way that was at one time second nature to us.

The American legal scholar and thinker John Powell has written and spoken quite extensively on race relations and the importance of group identification. Powell believes, "Being human is a 'process.' It's not something we are just born with; we actually learn to celebrate our connection, and learn to celebrate our love. If you suffer, it does not imply love, but if you love, it does imply suffering—to suffer with love and compassion, not to suffer against. And if we can hold that space big enough, we also have joy and fun even as we suffer. As a result, suffering will no longer divide us, and to me that's sort of the human journey."

I believe we can extrapolate Powell's idea of "shared suffering" as a way to celebrate connection, and apply it to why we seek out connection within the running community in general. Running is not a walk in the park—it demands commitment, persistence, and hard work. Most of us initially turned to running as a means to improve or maintain our physical health, but magically during that process, we discovered that there is an even bigger payoff when it comes to our mental well-being, and that feeling is certainly heightened the more we are connected to a broader running community.

But the main point I want to make is that what sets our running tribe apart from many of the other groups we belong to is the over-whelming sense of authenticity and vulnerability that characterizes our connections. As you read in the previous chapters in the runners' accounts of their experiences with injury and resilience, there is an almost endemic expression of openness and vulnerability that takes place in the community of runners. For sure, there are exceptions to the rule, but by and large we arrive at the sport with the desire to improve ourselves—not knowing whether or not we will ever arrive at that running nirvana. When it comes to the concept of embracing vulnerability, I think runners just get it—that insatiable desire that drives us to push through the physical and mental fatigue, and then to turn around and do the same thing again tomorrow. When you're engaged in that type of activity, it is next to impossible to maintain a veneer of invisibility. And I would argue that as a by-product of our engaging with other runners from this place of vulnerability, we ulti-mately arrive at our authentic self.

Once again I'll turn to the illuminating words of Jean Vanier: "A community is only being created when its members accept that they are not going to achieve great things, that they are not going to be heroes, but simply live each day with new hope, like children, in wonderment as the sun rises, and in thanksgiving as it sets. Community is only being created when they have recognized that the greatness of man is to accept his insignificance, his human condition . . . The beauty of man is in this fidelity to the wonder of each day."

BOYLSTON AND BACK AGAIN
THE AUTHOR'S STORY

We have arrived at a coalescence of this book, a place in which I expect we now have a deeper understanding of how by sustaining a running practice, we inadvertently unearth something inside us that in turn invites us to seek out connection with a broader running community.

Jazz great Eric Dolphy observed, "Once you play the music, it's in the air. It's gone . . . But when you record it, it comes back to haunt you sometimes." It's hardly surprising that it took an artist like Dolphy, a craftsman in the art of ephemeral melody, to beautifully express the bitter irony of the human condition—the belief that the memory we so desperately hang on to is what often tortures us the most. And for me, the enchantment of running lies in its ability to release that memory inside of us, and in so doing speak to our innate desire for connection and belonging—and to how, along the way, we find a pathway to empathy.

When I consider my running journey, there is one story that most clearly touches upon the three themes of this chapter: gravitation toward growth, building bridges and bonds, and authenticity through vulnerability. It's an inspirational example of how running not only brought me through adversity but also highlighted the healing power of the broader running community—those whom I affectionately refer to as my running tribe.

Throughout the book, I have made no secret of the fact that I am an addict in recovery, and over the years my belief in the therapeutic quality of running and my faith in the running community have been the cornerstones in keeping me from picking up that first drink or drug—what is certain to be the first step on the deathward spiral of addiction. But it wasn't until the early spring of 2013 that I first began to get a true understanding of how supportive the running community can be.

As a way to symbolically move beyond the tragedy of the Boston Marathon bombings, and in some way to vanquish the demons of my childhood trauma, I made the decision to return to Boston in the spring of 2014. And that's when my Type-A personality kicked into overdrive. If I was going back to Boston, it needed to be bigger, better, and more meaningful than ever before. I wanted to not only convince myself that I could run directly into what terrified me but also show everyone else that it was possible to live a life of joy and passion after surviving sexual violence. My plan was to run the Boston Marathon twice in the same day—once for me, and the second time for all the other survivors of childhood sexual abuse. By arriving at the finish line early on marathon morning and running the 26.2 miles to the official start, I would be symbolically "rewinding" all the trauma from my past and the previous year's race back to a better, safer place. And then, by turning around and running the 26.2 miles back into downtown Boston with the rest of the runners, I would be taking all of that pain and unhappiness and launching a new beginning. At this point, everything was about me, but I knew if this plan was to work, I would need to turn to the running community to make it happen.

After bouncing a few ideas off Mary-Anne, I decided that my

Double Boston would not only be about raising awareness of the issue of childhood sexual abuse but also about raising funds for the Gatehouse Treatment Centre in Toronto so that they could continue to do such needed work in our community.

I should probably let you know that up until this point, my disclosure process had been very public and very messy. I was on social media every day openly sharing what the impact of the disclosure of sexual trauma was like for me personally, and the ripple effect it had on my family in general. Time and again, it was my friends and complete strangers in the running community who reached out and supported me when I was at my lowest and most vulnerable. Literally, within minutes of my announcing on Facebook and Twitter that I would be running a Double Boston to raise five thousand dollars for the Gatehouse, my inbox was flooded with messages from friends and runners saying: "Are you crazy . . . Why only five thousand . . . Why not aim for fifteen thousand!" And so, with a big lump in my throat, I set up a fund-raising page with a target of fifteen thousand dollars. Before I hit the button to launch my site live, I stared at the empty fund-raising donation thermometer and felt an overwhelming feeling of doom and dread wash over me.

I started posting the link on Facebook and Twitter the next morning, and before lunchtime on that first day, over a thousand dollars had been pledged. Purely through family, friends, and hundreds of runners on social media, within two weeks I had reached my fifteen-thousand-dollar goal. I was completely shocked at the generosity and support of my online community; more important, I was humbled by the email and messages coming in from around the world from other survivors of sexual abuse. So many of you opened up to me about the trauma you've lived through, and how by running the Double Boston, I would be carrying you alongside me in spirit and resilience.

With only two weeks to go until the marathon, my fund-raising had tapered off because to be perfectly honest, I felt I had already reached my goal. That's when Mary-Anne suggested that I raise my target: "If people click on the link and see the donation thermometer at full, there is not much incentive for them to donate." So that's what I did, and once again I had that lump in my throat as I stared at the thermometer on my fund-raising page.

The final week leading up to Boston was consumed by working out the race logistics, printing out maps, and trying to get confirmation from the race director that I would even be allowed on the course early that morning due to the heightened security in place. Making things even trickier was the fact that due to the bombings the year before, runners were no longer allowed to carry backpacks or water hydration packs anywhere along the course or into the athletes' village.

In the final days before race morning, I was glued to the long-range forecast praying that it wasn't going to rain or be too cold. I knew it would be next to impossible for me to carry a change of clothes with me on the first leg of the marathon before arriving at the official staging area and corrals. The one thing I hadn't been expecting was the onslaught of media requests from all over North America. In the week leading up to the race, I did over fifty newspaper, radio, and television interviews—so much for arriving in Boston all tapered and rested!

The big unknown was whether or not Mary-Anne would be allowed to follow in a support vehicle for all or part of the first marathon; as a result, we made contingency plans just in case. The race director informed me that he suspected Mary-Anne wouldn't be permitted on the course, and that she would need to stick to the streets that parallel the race route. In either case, we arranged for a rental car to be picked up in downtown Boston on the evening before the marathon. While we were at the race expo on the Friday, we bumped into my dear friend Kathryn who just happened to be helping out at one of the booths. I asked her when she was flying back to Toronto, and she said just after lunch on marathon day. Over the past few months, I'd grown accustomed to reaching out for help, so I asked if she wanted to keep Mary-Anne company in the support vehicle. Kathryn didn't miss a beat: "Absolutely . . . What time do you want me?" I sheepishly said, "Four AM" and she replied, "Well, then . . . You better have coffee!"

Later that Friday evening, two days before the race, I was chatting with some runners on Twitter, and one of the gentlemen said he'd love to run Boston one day. I told him it was too bad I hadn't planned this better because I could've arranged for him to run the first leg of the marathon with me. He said, "Really?" and I thought that was the end of it. Thirty-six hours later I was walking around doing a little sightseeing in Cambridge when I got a message from this gentleman. It said, "Hi JP . . . It's Gines, the runner you were talking to on Twitter. I've driven down to Boston and I'm staying with a friend. What time do you want me on race morning?" I was dumbstruck, and turned the phone over to Mary-Anne so that she could read the message. She said, "That's totally cool!" I messaged Gines back and asked him to meet me at the finish line on Boylston at four thirty the next morning. He replied immediately with the following message, "Awesome. I'll be the guy wearing the red hat."

Later that afternoon Mary-Anne and I met up with a few of the other runners and their families to go to a matinee movie. It's become a Boston tradition that my buddy Almis and I have been doing for over ten years now. It's an excellent way to get off your feet and decompress a little before the marathon. As we were coming out of the movie and walking back to our respective hotels, I mentioned to one of the runners, Lisa, that this guy on Twitter had come into town to run the first leg of my double with me. That's when Lisa turned to her husband and said, "Greg, why don't you run with JP in the morning. It will give you something to do instead of just waiting around for me to finish the marathon." Turns out, Greg had never run more than twenty-one kilometers (thirteen miles) before, but I assured him that as soon as he felt wiped, he could hop into the support vehicle with Mary-Anne and Kathryn. And that was enough to seal the deal. It looked like the running community had come to my rescue yet again, and I wasn't going to be suffering out there in the dark all alone.

All that was left now was for me to try to grab a few hours of sleep before my 3 AM wake-up call. I lay back on the bed and responded to a backlog of Facebook and Twitter messages, and I posted my fund-raising link for the final time with the message, "Thanks everyone for all your support in my Double Boston effort. I'm heading off to bed now, and with less than 12 hours to go and a little over $4,000 to reach my fund-raising goal, looks like I'll fall a little short." And then it was lights-out for Mary-Anne and me.

When I was sitting at the desk eating my pre-marathon bagel in the wee hours of the next morning, Mary-Anne asked if any more donations had come in overnight. In all the stress of the morning, I had completely forgotten to check on the website. When I clicked on the link, my heart almost stopped, as I saw that my fund-raising thermometer was once again full. Unbeknownst to me, while I was sleeping, a few close friends in the running community took to social media with the following message: "Hey guys, JP is almost at his fund-raising goal, but he needs to get some sleep before he runs his double marathon. If you haven't already donated, now's the perfect time."

With the help of so many people, we were able to raise over twenty-five thousand dollars, and as result of all the media attention my run had generated, I was able to keep the issue of childhood sexual abuse front and center. But perhaps the greatest gift of all was hearing from the Gatehouse staff that calls requesting an intake interview for the survivor program were way up. To this day, the most important lesson I've learned from my disclosure process is the importance of acknowledging the freedom I received as a gift to be paid forward so that others can move beyond the childhood trauma that has defined their life for far too long.

Half an hour later, Kathryn was knocking on our hotel room door, and then the three of us made our way along the deserted downtown streets toward the finish line on Boylston. Standing shivering off in the darkness were the figures of two runners—Greg and Gines, both waiting for me to arrive. Although I had never met Gines before, I felt closer to him at that moment than I did to most of the people in my life. Here was someone who had left his young family behind and traveled a long way at his own expense, simply to support another runner he had met on Twitter.

We were getting ready to head out on our 26.2-mile trek to Hopkinton when all of sudden the bright lights of a truck came into focus. As it got closer, we could see it was a media truck, and before I knew it a reporter and a cameraman jumped out and said, "Are you the guy running the marathon twice today?" Looks like I had one more media interview to do before the run could get under way.

Greg, Gines, and I weaved our way out of downtown Boston along the race route, and at about the two-mile (three-kilometer) mark, we came across Mary-Anne and Kathryn waiting by the side of the road in the rental car. Much to our relief, it appeared as though they would be able to stay on the course with us for at least part of the way, so we arranged to have them meet us every two miles or so.

I can't tell you what a surreal experience it is to run the iconic Boston Marathon backward. If you were listening in on our conversation, you would hardly know that this was the first time the three of us had ever met, let alone run together. It felt as though these two men were my brothers, my best friends. We laughed and joked for the first hour and a half, and thankfully, that helped keep our mind off the bitter New England morning chill. But the funniest part of all was Greg, who was massively sleep-deprived yet totally gung-ho. He had gone out to the Red Sox game the night before, so he only managed to get three hours' sleep before meeting up with us. He kept saying, "I've only ever run a half marathon before, so all I want to do this morning is beat that distance, and then I'm hopping in the car." Greg wasn't wearing a GPS watch, so he had no idea how far he had already run. Gines and I gave each other a knowing glance because Greg had already run twenty-three kilometers (fourteen miles)! Greg was like a kid in the backseat of a car constantly asking "Are we there yet?" Gines and I kept saying, "Almost, just a few more minutes. We finally let Greg out of his misery at thirty kilometers (nearly nineteen miles), and according to Kathryn and Mary-Anne, he was super proud of what he'd accomplished that morning. To be honest, the second I saw Greg waiting for me in the dark that morning, he was already a hero in my heart.

Gines and I continued on until the thirty-six-kilometer (twenty-two-mile) mark, at which point the local police had closed down the road and asked that Mary-Anne pull off the course. I said my quick good-byes, gave everyone a big hug and kiss, and then made my way alone up the steep incline into Hopkinton and the official corrals. I finished the first half of my double marathon in a time of 4:09, and that left me about thirty minutes to wait in my corral for the official start of the marathon.

My legs felt fantastic as I began my second marathon of the morning. I made a promise to myself that I would enjoy the run back into Boston, and that I would stop along the way to take lots of selfies to post on Facebook, as well as respond to as many messages as possible from friends and other runners. After last year's stressful experience in Boston, Mary-Anne had asked that I carry my phone during the run so that she could send me text messages to check in with me along the way. I knew that she was a little anxious about being back at the marathon, but it felt as though she was especially eager to know where I was along the course. She kept telling me to look for her on a particular corner, located about one mile (1.6 kilometers) from the finish line. It wasn't until I came up to the meeting point that I realized why she had been so adamant that I keep an eye out for her. Standing beside Mary-Anne was my son, Noah, and his wife, Jackie. They had secretly flown into Boston the day before the race, and the three of them had planned to surprise me that morning. The moment I saw them, I broke down into tears, screamed for joy, and hugged Mary-Anne tighter than I'd ever done before. You see, it wasn't just me who had come this far—Mary-Anne had been with me all the way, just as she has been for almost thirty years. In my Double Boston, I may have been carrying the hopes and dreams of all the other survivors of childhood sexual abuse, but none of that would have been possible if it weren't for Mary-Anne helping me to see that strength within me.

I left my family on the corner and continued along the final mile of the Boston Marathon toward the epic finish line on Boylston. When I made the last turn onto the final stretch, every emotion possible coursed through me and out of me. I felt an immense sadness that had been my ever-present companion this past year slowly release from around my heart, and the words that I had heard so many people say to me—*I am proud of you*—echoed in my mind, but this time, for the first time I can ever remember, I believed in myself.

Now, if you've never seen the finishing straight along Boylston before, I want you to imagine a wide, expansive street lined with barricades along both sides holding back thousands of screaming spectators. Runners are off in their own little world, as they zone in on the finish line that lies tantalizingly close, yet so far away. Somewhere in the midst of this chaotic din, I heard someone screaming, "Hey JP . . . Way to go, brother!" I looked back to see Gines frantically waving at me as he lay draped over the metal barricade. I turned back and ran over to give him a huge hug. I barely knew who the hell this guy was, but in my books, he certainly was one of the most incredible people on the planet.

All that was left for me to do now was to finish the last hundred meters of this Double Boston . . . When I looked down at my watch, I realized I had crossed the finish line at 4:09 for the second time that day. What's even eerier is that I would later learn that I had crossed the finish line at exactly the same time, to the second, of the first explosion the year before.

As I sit here typing these words right now, I'm only just beginning to realize what a defining moment my Boston experience was in my life. It has taught me that most of the boundaries I brush up against are all in my mind, and that with the help of my family and my running family, I can find greatest within myself. Am I completely healed from my past trauma? Absolutely not. But what I am learning today is how to take that adversity and weave it into a life of hope, joy, and resilience.

REVERSE CULTURE SHOCK AND
FINDING YOUR HOME AGAIN
LEANNE'S STORY

After nearly four years in Africa, I reluctantly returned home to Toronto in September 2013. Well, I guess it was only partially reluctantly. I loved Malawi, but work had tapered off, things had gotten tough, and my boyfriend of two years and I decided we needed a change. Nothing was moving in Malawi—including me. An avid runner before I moved my life overseas, the stress and the years had taken a toll on me. I started off strong when I arrived, but the heat, the dust, the negative attention, and ultimately the laid-back lifestyle had turned me into a sedentary, unmotivated blob. Now back in Toronto, the prospect of running again excited and frightened me all at the same time.

Upon returning home, I busied myself worrying about my boyfriend's transition—he had never been to Canada before. I spent so much time trying to ensure he was transitioning well that I forgot about myself. By December, things had deteriorated, and my boyfriend gave up and went home. I wasn't mentally prepared for this. I wasn't prepared to face Canada on my own, as strange as that might sound. Reverse culture shock is like a sucker punch; you don't see it coming until it's too late, and it will knock you flat on your ass. Anxiety and loneliness showed up and wrapped their arms so tightly around me that I was suffocating within myself.

On one of the coldest January days we experienced in 2014, I somehow forced myself out the door to the local running store for the first night of a 5K clinic. I was underdressed and no longer equipped to deal with the extreme cold temperatures. Making it home after a mere twenty-five-minute run in the near minus-forty-windchill, I peeled off my tights and looked down at the white blotches of frostbite forming on my legs. I wrapped myself in a blanket, lay on my couch, and cried. I was angry. "Screw Canadian winter. Screw my boyfriend for giving up and leaving. Screw me for getting so out of shape. Screw everything."

But somehow I went again on Wednesday, and again on Sunday. It got easier . . . or I got better. The weather became more bearable. The hurt of being alone became less as I began to form bonds with the women and men in my group. Returning home, I had felt like I had no one. But on those group run days, I could put my mental suffering on a shelf and just run.

It's been well over a year and a half since that brutal "frostbitten day" in January 2014. In the months that followed, I ran through my inevitable breakup. I ran through the anxiety-ridden days I wanted to give up on home and escape back to the warm heart of Africa. I ran alone, and I ran supported by new running friends who dragged me out the door when I'd rather wallow in self-pity. I ran through another brutal Canadian winter. I ran across the finish line of a half marathon once again. I ran through it all. And through running . . . I found home.

A BROKEN HEART AND WHAT PROPELS YOU THROUGH YOUR PAIN
NANCY'S STORY

I believe that people are not only looking for a way to become or remain fit and healthy, but also looking for deeper connections through running. My group has challenged me to go beyond the dream I initially held for myself, which was to check a marathon off my bucket list. I never imagined it would become such an integral part of my life and my well-being.

I started training for my second marathon, Chicago, in June 2013, having just completed my first marathon a few months prior. Two weeks after the clinic started, I flew to Regina, Saskatchewan, to visit my family for a planned vacation. While I was flying back to Toronto, my thirty-four-year-old nephew Conrad had a massive heart attack. As I sat on the tarmac waiting to deplane, I received a message from my sister saying that she needed to speak with me. I knew immediately it was bad. She gave me the news that Conrad was in a coma and that the next twenty-four to forty-eight hours were critical. I asked if I should come home right away, and she suggested I wait until the next day, and that hopefully things would turn around.

I went for my regular Sunday-morning run the next morning, but I was numb with pain and fear for what may come to pass. I ended up cutting my run short as my hip was bothering me, and I was hyperventilating and crying. Later that evening, my brother called me to say that I needed to come home and that the prognosis was not good. I flew back to Regina the next morning and went directly to the hospital. When I saw my brother Darryl (Conrad's dad), I immediately knew that Conrad would not recover. Darryl is a retired police sergeant, so he had seen many things in his time on the force, and I could tell from his expression that he knew Conrad was essentially gone.

We spent the next week in hospital hoping for a miracle. I have always been the fixer in the family, but I could not fix this. On the Friday after he fell ill, we met with the team of doctors, and they told us that Conrad was brain-dead and that there was no chance he would recover. We could leave him on life support until he passed or we could remove him from life support. As a family, we made the most difficult decision we have ever had to make. Conrad passed away on Monday, July 15, on his sister's birthday. Fuck. He was everyone's favorite person, including mine. We had a very special bond, and I can't imagine loving him more if he'd been my own son, but I think only a parent can truly know the loss of a child.

It was completely devastating for all of us. On the last day of my vacation, Conrad had come to visit me before I flew back to Toronto, as he always did. We spent several hours having coffee, talking, and laughing our asses off. I told him all about my upcoming trip to Chicago, and he was so excited for me. I will be eternally grateful for that last morning and for the fact that our last words to each other were "I love you, Auntie," and "I love you too, baby boy" . . . I rarely called him Conrad . . . he was always my "baby boy."

In total, I spent a month in Regina with my family, and during this time my running community was a constant source of support from afar. My coach was in contact with me several times daily to check in on me, and because I wanted to continue to train while I was away, he even mapped out some routes for me so I could get my long runs in. He kept me sane and upright in a lot of ways.

When I returned to Toronto, my first run back was a long twenty-three-kilometer run. I was a mess, but I wanted to run and for about seven or eight kilometers I kept pace with my running group. My hip and calf started to bother me and I started to fall behind. I eventually lost everyone and had a massive anxiety attack and ended up actually getting lost. I was in pain, and my heart was broken, and I didn't know where I was. My coach was messaging me to find out where I was, and he ended up sending a car for me. I had run-walked twenty kilometers, most of it alone and in pain.

I continued to train and grieve very publicly, and my running group supported and accepted me for where I was at emotionally. I recall one night after running tempo loops, just sitting on the curb and sobbing my heart out. Three or four of the runners in my group came over and sat with me on the curb, and one by one they all told me about the losses they had suffered and how running helped propel them through their pain. They just propped me up, literally and figuratively. They constantly reached out to me—coffee dates, breakfast, lunch, dinner, movies, whatever. They would not let me isolate myself, and they were essentially my family in my time of need. I have no family in Toronto, so this is the group that supported me.

As the clinic progressed, my calf pain turned into an inflamed Achilles that was extremely painful and, as you probably know, not an easy injury to fix if you intend to keep on training while trying to heal. That just doesn't happen. But I had made a commitment to Conrad that I was going to run the marathon, so I kept going. I have an amazing chiropractor who treats athletes, and he was very honest with me and told me the only way to heal was to stop running. He also knows me well enough to know that I wasn't going to stop, so he treated me twice weekly during this time, and between him and my coach, we revised my training schedule. Initially I stopped doing hill training, as that was very hard on the Achilles. Later, I had to stop doing tempo/speed work.

By the time mid-September rolled around, I was only doing my long slow runs on the weekends. After each run, I would rest for a week and try to recover enough to do the next one. My long runs became very long, as my pace fell badly. I was convinced toward the end of the training that I would not be able to complete the marathon.

Chicago rolled around and we all traveled there on the Thursday before race day, including my coach who was also running the race. On the Friday, we went to the expo to pick up our kits. There were seven or eight of us, so we all split up and agreed to meet after we were done with our expo experience. I was standing in line to pay for some clothes when I looked at my phone and saw an email from someone who had what appeared to be the same name as my nephew, Conrad. I assumed it was my other nephew, who happens to have the same initials as Conrad. As I read the email, I realized it was someone writing it as though he or she were Conrad. And in this email, "Conrad" was telling me not to run the race because he didn't want to see me suffer. I almost dropped to my knees and threw up when I saw it was signed: "Love from your baby boy." My heart started to pound, and I began to hyperventilate. I paid for my purchases and fled the expo. I sat outside the expo sobbing and managed to compose myself by the time everyone met me. I was numb with pain, grief, and anger, and it made me more determined to finish the race.

Sunday morning eventually arrived, and we were about to disperse to our respective corrals, but I had to step away from the group, as I was experiencing anxiety again and I had a moment of extreme fear. I kept thinking, *What if that email was a sign that I'm actually not supposed to run the race? What if something bad happens? What if I tear my Achilles? What if I am one of those people who drops dead right after they finish?* These thoughts just freaked me out. So I did some deep breathing and recommitted myself to Conrad, knowing full well that he would realize how much this meant to me, and that he would want me to do this, if not for him, then at least for myself. I said to myself, *If I drop dead at the finish line, at least I will drop dead doing something I love, for someone I love.*

I was worried about my anxiety attacks because I had them on every long run after Conrad died . . . every fucking time . . . it was brutal. I kept thinking, *How am I going to stave off the panic attacks?* I made another decision right there—I decided I would smile for the entire race and make eye contact with fellow runners and people in the crowd. And I went for it. In every race picture, there is a smile on my face, some big, some more of a grimace, but it worked!

Although my goal was just to finish, secretly I was hoping I could finish it in less than six hours. I crossed the finish line at 5:58:09! These are numbers that will be etched on my brain forever. I was so happy and exhausted. I had done it.

I can't begin to express how much my community carried me through this period and even afterward. Being surrounded by such amazing people reaffirmed my faith in humanity. So many people took my heart in the palm of their hands, and carried it ever so gently across that finish line.

DOGS AND PEOPLE BOTH RUN IN PACKS
JOHN'S STORY

There certainly is a meditative and healing aspect to running on one's own, but having said that, I credit the rise in group running to the social aspects of it, both for the camaraderie and for the benefit of sharing each other's learning and experiences. However, one of the strongest reasons is for the familial bonds that form between runners. That is what's kept me running with my group, and that's what I've seen attract others as well.

I began my running obsession by joining a running clinic. I wasn't very physically active before, and had a tendency to feel shy about not being good at a sport. These two traits fed off each other to the point where I had avoided trying new physical activities out of fear of being judged for my lack of ability, so joining a running clinic was a big step in taking me out of my comfort zone. More aptly put, I pushed myself out of my comfort zone as a way to deal with big changes and painful experiences in my life.

In the months before I started running, I went through some difficult change. My beloved dog passed away. One of my closest friends lost his battle with cancer, and my wife left me. I was struggling with these while also trying to prove myself in a new job, and the pressure was becoming too much. I distinctly remember thinking to myself that I'd need to do something active to cope; otherwise, I'll end up using alcohol as an escape. While I was trying to figure out what that "active something" was, I saw a group of runners and a sign for the Goodlife Toronto Marathon.

I pushed myself to visit the running store by my home, and met someone who would later become one of my running coaches for several clinics, and also one of my closest friends. That was sixteen months ago. Since then, I've met a lot of great people, and have formed some great friendships.

In talking with others, I've found that many people were in a similar boat as I was when they started running. There are so many changes and challenges happening in everyone's life, so much so that people need a coping tactic and a group of friends they can escape with. One of the beautiful aspects of a long slow run is that you get to spend a lot of time with friends running at a pace at which you can talk to each. This is one of the primary factors to which I attribute the rise in the number of running groups.

I've heard the term *running tribe,* but I've always been a fan of *running pack.* I suppose it's obvious that I'm a dog person! The word *tribe* or *pack* addresses the non-running component of a running group. This includes the social aspect, the post-run brunches, the group destination race vacations, the forming of friendships, the demonstrations of loyalty, and the mutual support.

I recently went on a destination run to an out-of-town trail race with some runners from my clinic. We rented five rooms side by side in a motel in Huntsville. For many of us, it was our first trail race. We ran the race at different paces in smaller groups, but had several culinary adventures together in this small town, and stayed up late, crashing at one motel room and playing board games until we couldn't keep our eyes open any longer.

When it comes to a clear advantage of the running community's online presence, it is definitely having a vast online library of resource material. Be it training guides, biomechanics, nutrition, gear, or tips, there is a wealth of knowledge just waiting at our fingertips.

The downside can come when people feel demotivated reading about others' successes, or lash out at them. I've heard some slower runners grumble about the charts and stats posted by a faster friend. I've also heard faster friends question the performance of another fast friend. But I guess all this is to be expected with any popular sport where folks are competitive.

BEING VULNERABLE ONLINE IS
A LOT EASIER THAN IT IS IN PERSON
CHRISTA'S STORY

I like to belong . . . in my own way. I don't necessarily like to conform, so groups of any kind are not a place I feel entirely comfortable. I suspect that if I were more local to my team, I would develop closer bonds to my teammates, and that would make it easier and more comfortable to be part of the group.

I further suspect that being vulnerable in person is a lot different from being vulnerable digitally. Electronic vulnerability, I can do for some reason, whereas I don't seem to have the courage it takes to struggle and sweat and slog out a run in person. A person's ability to handle the tough stuff is very telling, and some days I am afraid I wouldn't measure up to their expectations, so I run it out on my own. I run periodically with one or two close girlfriends, near my home. It is only with these women that I feel safe to suffer, or to be weak and fail. Essentially the role of my tiny running group of three is to not only share the kilometers but also share the deep things that don't find the light of day anywhere else except for out on the run.

My larger team, which is non-local to me, serves to inspire me to be better. I am proud of their achievements and success from a distance in most cases, and aspire to earn their respect through the work I do at becoming better at my sport. I am a cheerleader. I have always been better at appreciating others' abilities and achievements than my own, and I am pretty vocal about that. I love to watch others crush goals and perform well. I get a lot of satisfaction from supporting people, and I think this is driven by the nurturer in me.

NO RUNNER IS AN ISLAND
EMILY'S STORY

Not another running injury! Oh, at first I *hated* social media. Self-ishly, I didn't want to see other people running and enjoying it. My entire Twitter feed is people talking about running, and it made me recoil and avoid looking at it.

In hindsight, I should have reached out more. Everyone is so sup-portive, and so willing to help—the "no man is an island" stance is definitely the one I'll take next time. The community really makes you realize that you're not the only one who's gone through some-thing strenuous and difficult, and that you certainly don't have to do it alone. Just last night I went for an eight-kilometer run (shhh . . . don't tell my orthopedic surgeon), and while I was almost in tears at the beginning, there were so many of the old, friendly, familiar run-ning faces there that I couldn't stay sullen for long. Everyone was so happy to see me, wanting to check in on how my knee felt. And some were even running slower than I know they wanted to just to stay with me. It was amazing.

A LOVE–HATE RELATIONSHIP WITH SOCIAL MEDIA
MARA'S STORY

I must admit, I have a love–hate relationship with social media. On the one hand, it can be really inspiring to see so many people working to stay fit and healthy. On the other hand, social media lends itself to the need for external validation; so much so that I wonder if some of us would continue to run if we weren't able to get the validation of posting an Instagram photo or an update on a blog. I am very cognizant of this, and am the first to admit that I've fallen prey to the need for external validation through social media. When this happens, I usually try to take a little break from posting to get back to understanding why I run in the first place.

And in the end, I really do love seeing so many people engage in running. Admittedly, it can be hard when you see folks running crazy amounts of miles at super-impressive speeds (I am a slow turtle runner!), but part of my own healing process is learning to celebrate others without comparison, and to be happy and comfortable at the pace I set for myself.

NO PENGUIN GETS LEFT BEHIND
JOANNE'S STORY

My running tribe is probably the main reason that I am even still running, and the reason that I was able to push the limits of my conceived boundaries. I first started running when my youngest was a toddler, and I was thirty-eight. I desperately needed something for myself, and so I started with running around the block, after reading about using a run–walk ratio. It was really hard, and I didn't actually know anyone who was a runner, so I was desperate to find a running group. However, when I checked into groups, they were all faster than I was, and their group runs were farther than I was running at that time.

A few months later, I got up my courage and approached the head of the Toronto Penguins. The group was doing an out-and-back route, but I couldn't run fast enough to finish the route on time, so Glenn ran with me at my slowpoke pace, and we turned around before the halfway point so that we could finish with the others.

My new running tribe embraced me with enthusiasm, and in my shiny-eyed wonder I was overwhelmed with amazement at the races they were running. I listened with fascination to conversations about half marathons and marathons. I was still trying to get to 5K! That was my only goal, as I couldn't imagine running any farther. The thought of running a marathon was so unrelatable to me that I equated it with training to become an astronaut. It was not something that I thought I could ever do. I was hooked, though, after my first 5K race, and gradually worked my way up to a marathon, with the support of my Penguins, whose motto is "Penguins never leave a Penguin on the course." I loved the fact that they would wait around after a race until every last Penguin had finished.

My schedule got really busy over time, and eventually I had to give up my actual group runs, but I kept in touch with people online. My tribe grew over time, and started to include people who I saw at races regularly, and who eventually became friends. My tribe helped me move from marathons to ultramarathons, and they are always there to offer sympathy, support, and sometimes a good kick in the pants if I feel sorry for myself. Without my running tribe, I never would have learned so much about myself or developed the courage to step past my self-imposed limitations. One of the nice things about an online community is that they become your virtual tribe. They are ones to whom you are accountable; they know what it's like to train for something, the commitment it takes, the aches and pains of training, and the celebration of the human spirit when you are out running.

Running has completely changed my life, and given me so many adventures, including my "hurricane" marathon, when Hurricane Sandy hit Washington the day after the Marine Corps Marathon and I couldn't leave the city. I ran the marathon with my best running buddy Mau, and we were stuck in the hotel with a few other runners and a skeleton staff. It was scary being in the hurricane, but also the only time that I got to wear my pajamas all over a hotel!

I USED TO THINK ONLY SUPERHEROES DID THAT KIND OF THING
LISA'S STORY

The running community has shaped me into a better runner in that they helped me throw my limits out the window. I never thought I would be racing ultras or training for a BQ. My tribe, especially my club—Run It Fast Club—opened up those possibilities for me. I had no idea there were runners who ran marathons every weekend or did multiple hundred-milers in a year. Once you see that others can do things you thought were impossible or unimaginable, you definitely start thinking bigger. I definitely would not have run twenty-three marathons and ultras if not for them. Before I joined Run It Fast, I thought only superheroes did that kind of thing. Now it seems perfectly normal to me to think that big, whether it's distance or time goals.

When it comes to the intersection between running a social media, a few of the disadvantages are the traps it can lead to, most notably the Fear Of Missing Out and Comparison Syndrome! I keep saying that I'm going to race less, but I see everyone having fun at races and getting great bling, and before you know it I'm signing up for another race! It gets addicting, and seeing race medals and PRs on Instagram, Twitter, and Facebook all the time makes it hard to resist.

I have also had to give myself some serious lectures to stop comparing myself to other runners. It can be a little disheartening to work really hard to get a sub-4 marathon and then see someone crank out

3:30s as if it were a jog in the park. I have to remind myself that "fast" is relative, and that what I have accomplished so far is awesome. I still do have **PR** & **BQ** envy sometimes, so I try to channel it into dedication toward my goals, but I would be lying if I said I wasn't envious of other runners' abilities at times.

In September 2013, I was diagnosed with ovarian cancer. I was scared out of my mind at what the doctor would tell me after surgery, and terrified at the thought of chemotherapy. My two biggest supporters whom I leaned on during that time were friends I made through running. And the rest of my online running community made up a huge support and prayer group during this time. They offered to take me to chemo or bring me dinner if they lived nearby. They checked on me to see how I was doing. They sent me flowers and small gifts to cheer me up. They encouraged me to keep running and distracted me when I was sad about not being able to run or race. They celebrated with me when I beat cancer. And they celebrated with me when I returned to racing.

But it isn't only during the bad times that the running community rallies around each other. I have been filled with joy to see my friends marry and have children and watch them grow. I have truly been blessed by my running tribe. I have been lucky to travel to different states to meet tribe members or meet them when they come to California. Now it's very rare that I race and don't know someone else who will be there. Running has made the world smaller in some ways but also opened it up, and the running community is a big part of that.

EVERYONE NEEDS HER TRIBE
HEATHER'S STORY

Runners are looking for the social support and connectedness that they get from a club or crew, and that often arrives in the motivation, inspiration, and conversation you get from being a member of a running group. I also know running is accessible. No matter your experience or socioeconomic status, with a pair of running shoes you can head out on the pavement or trails, and you are a runner.

When deciding whether or not a particular running club is for you, it's definitely important to give clubs and crews a test run. Chat with other members while out on the run. Go to the run knowing what you expect and what your goals are. You might also consider searching the club or crew online. Investigate their routes, paces, goal races, and goals as a crew. If these align with yours, then they definitely sound worth checking out.

In 2013, when I established Tribe Fitness, my goal was to unite the Toronto fitness community in "sweating for social good." Using City Place in the downtown core as its hub, Tribe Fitness provides free run, yoga, and cycling experiences, as well as leading wellness services and knowledge that promote fun, and healthy active living.

From the beginning, Tribe has been about using fitness as a means to build community. It is a place for people, no matter their experience, to feel included, to be seen and heard, and to know that they matter. A memorable moment was certainly at the start, maybe a month into our run crew. It was post-run, and I had left my cell phone on; suddenly, my Twitter alerts went bananas. In about fifteen minutes, I had over seventy-nine tweets to our Tribe account. It was obvious from my phone alerts that Tribe members who had been out on the run were sharing and connecting. My husband questioned who was texting me so much, so I checked my phone, had a huge smile on my face, and responded, "It's the Tribe." That was the first moment that I realized this has nothing to do with me, and everything to do with community.

I'm motivated by a couple of different things. The first is my own goals. I grew up in an active family, so physical activity has always been a part of my life. I enjoy setting goals and working toward them. The process of setting a goal, facing the challenge head-on, and then of course feeling the success is great motivation to do it again. My first Ironman 70.3 was certainly this experience. Challenging myself through months of training and then of course on race day. Crossing the finish line, holding my sister's hand as we raced and finished together was an amazing accomplishment.

I am also motivated by the Tribe community—from our Couch to 10K Runners to our Marathon Crew. I am motivated and inspired by people who are focused, driven, and challenge themselves to be a better version of themselves—no matter their goal, imagining that they can be something different, something better, and supporting them as they work toward it . . . well, that's a huge motivation.

UNRAVELING INTO FRIENDSHIP
LEANNE'S STORY

There has always been a metaphysical exchange when I run—it has seen me through the some incredibly challenging times. Whether I feel emotionally, physically, or spiritually broken, I continue to run. If I run with hurt, pain, and brokenness, somehow I come back with a sense of accomplishment, strength, and a will to overcome. One such difficult time was finding out that my daughter had been abused. What unraveled throughout this part of my journey still has me bewildered and has forever changed me.

So it is here, during this phase of my life, in this state of mind, that I decided I was still going to train for and run my first marathon. I decided to go out of my comfort zone and join a running group. I am a very strong, independent person, so I could have done the training on my own, but I didn't want to. I wanted the company of others on my long runs. I had no idea how important this group would become to me.

I cannot fully express my gratitude to the very first running group I had the privilege of running with. We were a group of about seven runners. We ran three times a week together. There was an immediate sense of safety for me. I was going through the worst time in my life, and I could run free with these strangers. I began to share my heart with one or two of them. On our long runs, I opened up about some of the pain I was experiencing. At this time, there was no one else in my life I felt I could talk to. These people (now friends) were separate from my everyday life. They didn't know me, or anyone else associated with me. I had a place where I could share my heart freely and be completely accepted. This was not all one-sided. Collectively, we shared our lives. Running was our common thread.

I have now been running with this group for approximately two and a half years. It is the most inclusive group I've ever been a part of. Everyone is accepted and welcomed. We are all there to learn more and share our experiences. Friendships continue to form, and the group as a whole celebrates with one another, no longer just with running but with many aspects of our lives crossing over.

COMRADES FROM NEAR AND FAR
SIAN'S STORY

Running is one of those sports that can be both solitary and social at the same time. It is also very global and incredibly inclusive—anyone can run a marathon; you don't need much skill, just heart and determination. This is what brings the running community together because no matter what language, religion, or race, if you run, you can understand any other person who runs. Runners are everywhere, and with social media growing at the rate it is, it's the most obvious platform to create running groups. The fact that these groups can span across continents is testimony to the power of the run.

Every runner loves to talk about running, to share his or her experience, to moan about the pain, the black toenails, the cramps, and to get advice and share advice with others.

The running community is one that lives to run, and this means getting others involved, motivating, and inspiring others. A runner has experienced the joy that running can provide and wishes to share that with everyone who will listen—and even those who won't! In South Africa, running groups or clubs are integral to our running culture, as they provide a home base and support network as well as training groups in local areas. Running clubs are also responsible for organizing a lot of our local races, and it's how runners give back and create a culture of responsibility and ownership.

When it comes down to it, pretty much every runner is part of the tribe. We all get it—the early mornings, battling heat or cold to get in those miles needed for the next race, or even just feeling your feet pounding the earth, heart pumping, lungs burning; it's a feeling we all get, and it's what draws us back every day.

As the museum curator of the Comrades Marathon, I am privileged to witness the spirit of the international running community first-hand. I have not run the race myself, but it is the most humbling and life-affirming experience to watch. I have grown up with this race; family members have run it, and I have been involved since I was a child, either as a supporter or volunteer, and now finally as a staff member. Getting to meet the runners and then seeing them cross that finish line every year is the most amazing feeling, and to see that change in expression as they realize what they have just accomplished, well, that has to be the one of the most beautiful sights in the world. It is awe inspiring. Watching the large pace groups, which we refer to as buses, come in is a phenomenon of its own. I can't even begin to describe the feeling of witnessing two thousand runners entering the stadium together, knowing they have just run ninety kilometers of hard terrain, holding each other up, supporting each other every step, and crying and laughing together. It is just otherworldly to see so much love, so much true humanity—the good part of what we are as a species.

Part of my job is running (pun intended) social media pages, and with that, I see both the positive and the negative. I work for a marathon, and I run. It's obvious I love running, but being on both sides as an organizer and as a runner, I see all the good and all the bad. The bad is we runners are rather demanding a lot of times, and once we find something to complain about, man do we complain! We can blow simple situations way out of proportion, and it can be detrimental when a negative thread keeps on going—it just breeds negativity. Also, a lot of runners will happily voice complaints on social media, but then won't think to send these complaints directly to the organizers. On a positive note, social media has immense power, as a serious issue aired on these platforms can also help to ensure correct attention will be paid, and the issue fixed.

In terms of online communities, we all live everywhere, so when the poor guy having to run in minus ten degrees is unsure, his running mate living on the other end of the world running in a balmy twenty-four degrees will be a good motivation. It also opens us up to new running opportunities and experiences. Online communities allow for this; runners share their experiences and grow the interest in different races, thus growing running.

In running, we become family. It's not only the run that is important; so too is each person's well-being and happiness. This is why running is the most beautiful of all sports—we compete against ourselves more than against each other, and as such, it becomes about lifting each other higher and farther. In many ways, running is just a conduit for our real humanity to show through.

A REASON TO DRAG MY BUTT OUT OF BED
ON A SUNDAY MORNING
SUE'S STORY

Running is very challenging physically. For new runners, it's a daunting task mentally too. The way that many running stores structure their programs and running groups makes this mentally overwhelming task more manageable. If you start with a "Learn to Run" clinic, as I did, you realize that you are not suffering alone. There is great comfort in struggling with others. You know then that it's not just you. I think it is in our nature to think that everyone else is doing well, or is great, or better than us. We are always comparing ourselves to others, in all aspects of our lives. Finding the right group and a common goal is very comforting and encourages you to keep going. My running tribe is the very reason why I haul my lazy butt out of bed on a Sunday morning when I would much rather just sleep in.

I've moved through the clinics, from "Learn to Run" to 5K, to

10K, and am now in the half-marathon group. I only started running, for the first time ever, in January and through that freezing-cold February. This new group is very challenging, as some of the ladies are really good runners who have run for a long time. What made a huge impression upon me is that even these seasoned runners, who are way better than I am, think it's really hard. They too are sweating, and panting, and pushing themselves. This whole running thing is very hard, yet they keep doing it and have done so for years. That impressed me, and has made me realize that, no matter how hard it is while you are doing it, it never occurs to you to ever give up. That's huge! Overcoming that mental barrier shows how strong you can become if you just keep moving forward.

The advantages of the online running community are the ease of communication and the availability of information, which is often quite motivational. It's also the sharing of the journey and the support that you feel if you are struggling with similar issues, or just plain struggling with issues of your own. What keeps you moving forward is knowing that you are not alone and that others—who have their own struggles—are able to overcome them or better manage them through the shared enjoyment of running.

CARRYING US TOWARD THE FINISH LINE
GINES'S STORY

With running, there is a draw to a sense of community, and that brings a sense of belonging. It's a place where running communities, groups, and clinics don't judge on ability but are simply grateful that you are out and joining them.

My most memorable running experience took place at the finish line of a fifty-kilometer race in the American Midwest. Less than a mile to the finish, a runner from my group collapsed with intense cramps. People ran over to help him up to his feet, but as he tried to jog, he fell again. A group of us linked arms and carried him to the line. At that moment, no one said, *Hey let's get him to the finish line* or *Let's go help him out* or even *Can you help him?* It was just something we all felt inside of us to act upon at the same time. To me, that's the heart of the running community.

The connections to be made through running are incredible. As a matter of fact, if it were not for the running community both online and in person, I would not be writing this. I met the author of this book you're reading right now online, and eventually met in person after a couple of years at the Boston Marathon. It was the year Jean-Paul did his Double Boston, and I had the pleasure of joining him for part of his first leg. It's a prime example of how running brings two people together from across the globe. Two people who share a commonality and a similar passion for running. If it were not for running and these communities, this connection may never have happened.

BIRDS OF A FEATHER
LISA'S STORY

Have I found my tribe . . . Well, I'm not sure yet. I have just found myself with my first running buddy ever. We have been running together weekly for the last seven months, and it has become hugely important to me. I guess I'd have to say that we've got our own little duo tribe, and we love it. People really lay themselves bare on the run. Maybe it's the lack of direct eye contact, or maybe it's the freedom of the open space. For whatever reason, running alongside someone you trust, even if you barely know him or her yet, allows you to open up and let things out. It's like a therapy and a sweat session all rolled into one!

THEY WILL ALWAYS BE IN MY LIFE
LUCIA'S STORY

I started running after the birth of my third baby simply because it was the easiest form of fitness. I would either hire a sitter or take him to the day care at the gym. I loved the freedom of being able to lace up my shoes and run out the door. I could go whenever I wanted, rather than racing to catch an aerobics class—something I was still doing; it was the '90s after all! It didn't take long for running to become my me-time, my escape from everything I had to do. It was something I savored. I got high on the endorphins almost immediately—freedom and exhilaration!

Life can be a lonely place, and I think people crave community. There is so much in our world that can make us feel alone, so it makes sense that innately we want to reach out and connect with others. Sharing a run, which very often evolves into sharing tidbits of our lives, is such an easy and effective way to not feel alone. I've actually had people tell me that they see running groups go by and they see the laughter and camaraderie, and they want to be part of it. Deep down no one wants to be alone.

When it comes to running groups, I think people should just jump in and join the group; you never know what will evolve. You don't know whose path you may cross; you don't have to be the same age/gender/speed to connect with someone. Give it a chance, be open, and simply let it be. Enjoy the runs and you never know where it will take you.

For the past few years, I've had the honor of leading a Women's Run Clinic at my local running store. The moment that I cherish the most occurred about two years ago when the girls in my group presented me with a beautiful Christmas card and gift, and, most important, shared with me for the first time how I had impacted each of their lives.

I never expected to receive anything back when I decided to volunteer to lead this group; I had simply wanted to give a little something back to the running community I'd been part of for almost ten years. But suddenly a group of twenty women were telling me how much they loved me and the group we had all built together. It was so unexpected, and reduced me to tears almost instantly. I never realized how powerful my words and actions were toward them, and it was such a reminder of how our daily interactions with others can affect them in ways we may not know. Kind words, encouragement, support, positivity—they are never ever wasted. I was and remain humbled by the love and respect I get back from this incredible group of women.

It may be a little selfish, but as our group has become so supportive, deep and meaningful friendships have evolved. I could never turn my back on that. I love these women, and there's no question of me continuing to keep them in my life. In addition, I've seen that as their confidence in themselves grows, so does their drive to push their own boundaries. More and more of them are beginning to train for their first marathon or to reach for a new PB. Three years ago I heard a lot of *I can't*, and now I'm hearing more of *I'd like to try*. I love bearing witness to that growth, so of course I'm going to stay around to help them reach those goals!

Epilogue

We carry within us the wonders we seek without us.
—Eric Butterworth

A week ago, I set aside some time in my busy schedule to sit down at the computer so that I could write this epilogue. I had all the intentions and expectations of extrapolating some kernels of wisdom shared by so many contributors to this book. Having read over the chapters and the stories contained within, I was hoping to pull together or in some way distill the beauty that running brings into our lives.

But as is so often the case, fate had other plans in store. Throughout the pages of this book, it's been my intention to express the primal healing and transformative experience that running brings to those who surrender to its alchemy. And as so many other voices in this book have echoed, our faith in sustaining and nurturing a running practice opens the door for some truly remarkable and inspiring people to enter our life.

To say that I have been blessed by my running community is indeed a great understatement. My life has become ever the richer by surrounding myself with a patchwork community of runners—supporters, role models, community builders, inspiring truth seekers, and rogue characters alike.

But when I look back on all the people who have touched my life through running, none has left a more caring and gentle footprint than my dear friend Diane. You may remember Diane's story from earlier in the book: She spoke about how difficult it was for her to stay positive through her prolonged injury. I can still remember the day her story arrived in my inbox, and the messages back and forth over the following days. I've known Diane for a few years now, but I had never seen her open herself up with such intense vulnerability. In her story, she shared how conflicted she felt about being perceived as self-centered, as she was preoccupied with a running injury while her husband was battling a recent cancer diagnosis. It's a dark, lonely place that most runners have found themselves in. It's a place ripe with fear, as we stand bare, having the thing that comforts us most, the passion that defines us, suddenly taken from us. As painful as it was for Diane to write her story, we can only imagine how even more painful it was for her to share it with us.

So it's with the heaviest of hearts that I share the following news with all of you. Three days ago, the unimaginable happened. Early in the morning while Diane was walking on the sidewalk near her workplace, she was struck by a tire that had dislodged from a dump truck passing on the street. The force and velocity of the two-hundred-pound tire struck Diane in the head, and the trauma proved to be fatal. It feels impossible to come to terms with such a random, senseless death. In a fraction of a second, we all lost one of the most beautiful and caring people we could ever hope to meet. A family now grieves the loss of a wife, a mother, and a grandmother. How you put all of that sorrow into words, I will never know.

Diane, like me, was an early-morning runner, so we chatted most mornings when we got home from our respective runs. Over the years, what started out as a casual friendship over social media blossomed into a very personal and supportive relationship. Diane was one of the people who literally held my hand through some of the darkest days of my life, and by way of her eternal optimism, irreverent sense of humor, and unwavering empathy, she taught me to see the beauty in myself, and to expect more of myself.

I received the devastating news of Diane's accident as Mary-Anne and I were driving down to Rochester, New York, so that I could compete in the marathon just this past weekend. During the next twelve hours, we learned the extent of Diane's injuries, and that she eventually succumbed. I barely slept that night as my mind tried to process what had occurred. I wasn't sure if I would be able to race that day, but I decided to write Diane's name on my race bib and get it done like I knew she would want me to.

As luck would have it, my stomach started acting up at thirty kilometers, and I was convinced I would need to drop out of the race. I walked for a few minutes, and that's when I noticed the following message that someone had chalked on the road for another runner— GO DIANE, GO! WE LOVE YOU! I couldn't believe what I was seeing, and I took it as a sign that I was meant to push through the discomfort and finish this marathon for Diane. And that's what I did.

I've spent the better part of this past year working on this book, and as I listen to the joys, heartache, and love that populate the stories submitted by hundreds of runners from around the world, one common theme winds its way throughout: To the casual observer, running may not appear rational. It certainly does not speak to the rational part of our brain. In fact, if we knew at the outset the immense effort and transformative power required when entering into a running practice, most of us would cower in a dark corner. But that still does not change the fact that we are entranced by everything running brings to us, and reveals within us.

I would have to agree with the entrepreneur and inspirational speaker Chip Conley, who once said, "Curiosity is the opposite of depression"—not "happiness" as many might believe. In its purest form, running is a beautiful expression of our innate curiosity. It's an enchanting journey to awaken something inside of us that carries us through adversity while uniting us in self-discovery. And come to think of it, where is curiosity found but on the ever-so-precarious edge, that border between fear and exhilaration? Granted, it may not always feel like the safest place to be, but I challenge you to find a place in which you feel more alive.

One of my favorite writers, Elizabeth Gilbert, says: "When you come to the end of yourself, that's where all the interesting things start." And for me, that's what running is all about—it opens us to possibility, adversity, and exploration. Each of us who makes a commitment to nurturing a running practice makes the most precious investment we have—an investment of our ever-dwindling time. We make a conscious effort to carve out a part of our day to do what I believe to be the most majestic of all human quests—running into yourself.